Community Participation in School Education

Community Participation in School Education

D.P. Singh
Ritu Mor

SHIPRA

ISBN: 978-81-7541-669-7

First Published in India in 2013

Community Pariticipation in School Education

Published by:
SHIPRA PUBLICATIONS
H.O.: LG 18-19, Pankaj Central Market, Patparganj,
I.P. Ext., Delhi-110092, Tel: 91-11-2223 5152, 2223 6152
Br.Off.: 4617/18, Ansari Road, Darya Ganj,
New Delhi-110002, Tel: 6594 6453, 9810522367
E-mail: info@shiprapublications.com
www.shiprapublications.com

Preface

Community participation in school education in India has always been thought as an integral part of the educational set up. The First Education Commission in 1966 clearly spelt out the need of decentralization of school education and involvement of local bodies in the processes related to school improvement. According to the Commission, the immediate goal was to associate communities with the schools in their locality. Community participation as a primary strategy for ensuring decentralization in school education got a major boost with the adoption of National Policy on Education in 1986. The NPE 1986 visualized direct community involvement in the form of Village Education Committees (VECs) for management of elementary education. The Policy envisaged people's involvement and participation in educational programmes at the grass-root levels as very important. The Policy viewed Village Education Committees as bodies that could ensure participation of every child in every family in primary education either formally or through non-formal means. The Programme of Action (POA) 1992 further strengthened the Village Education Committees by providing that the State Government will lay down general guidelines regarding the constitution of village education committees and establish norms of accountability in respect of the Heads of these institutions. The major responsibility of the village education committee was to operationalise micro level planning and school mapping in the village through a systematic house to house survey and discussions with the parents. The 73rd and 74th Constitutional Amendments in 1992 also provided a fillip for decentralisation activities and facilitated the transfer of power and participation of the local self-government institutions or the Panchayati Raj Institutions (PRIs). The PRIs have also, been delegated responsibilities with regard to location and relocation of existing primary and upper schools on the basis of micro planning and school mapping. Under these Acts, decentralisation of school management to grassroots level bodies is an important policy initiative. District Primary Education Programme (DPEP) one of the most comprehensive programmes launched in 1994 with international assistance from World Bank and European Union was designed primarily as a decentralized program to address local needs and circumstances by involving local stakeholders. The communities were required to establish Village Education Committees (VECs) under DPEP. Local groups including Parent Teacher Associations (PTA) and Mother Teacher Councils (MTC) were also encouraged to participate in VECs. The Lok Jumbish (LJ) and Shiksha Karmi Programmes (SKP) launched in 1994 stressed on mobilizing the village community to take responsibility to universalise and deliver quality education. The positive impact of the LJ and SKP served as a model for designing innovative approaches for community involvement in all educational activities of a village school in the country.

Sarva Shiksha Abhiyan (SSA) launched in the year 2002, aims to Universalize Elementary Education (UEE) through people's involvement and participation. SSA assigns greatest importance to systematic mobilization of the community and creation of an effective system of decentralized decision making. It calls for community ownership of school-based interventions through effecting decentralization. It puts a great deal of emphasis on the civil society for ensuring the effectiveness and viability of our school education. Institutions such as Village Education Committee/School Management and Development Committee/ Ward Education Committees have been set up at village or school level in almost all the states to ensure community participation in the school education system. The Right to Education Act 2009 is another historic step which recognizes the role of local governance in school education. The Act specifies that a School Management Committee (SMC) shall be constituted for every school to monitor and oversee its working, and to plan and facilitate its overall development with representation of parents, teachers and community and local authority members, as may be prescribed by the appropriate State government.

The above background provides the necessary justification for this volume which derives its academic arguments primarily from the findings of a research study aimed at evaluating the functioning of Village Education Development Committees in Punjab. The study has tried to know how far these committees have been able to achieve their goals. What are the views of the people about these bodies? What problems and constraints do these committees face? What can be the mechanisms by which the functioning of Village Education Development Committees can be strengthened? In this light, the volume has been divided into eight major chapters. Chapter one tries to conceptualize community participation apart from presenting an evolution of the idea of community participation in India mentioning different milestones in terms of various commissions and committees set up by the Government from time to time for decentralization of school education. Chapter two attempts to give a brief overview of some of the education related programmes implemented in different states by both the central as well as respective state governments for facilitating a congenial environment for participation of community people in the day to day governance of village school. Chapter three presents an elaborate review of researches done on various aspects of participatory governance of village schools in India and abroad. Chapter four provides the experiences of decentralized management of village schools across some of the Indian states. Chapter five is devoted to the communitisation of school education in the state of Punjab by presenting a comprehensive account of the Government Guidelines regarding the working of Village Education Development Committees (VEDCs). Chapter six present an elaborate account of the process of formation, composition and functions of VEDCs apart from knowing the socio-economic profile and awareness level of the Committee members. Chapter seven present an overview of the general facilities available in the sampled schools apart from examining the contribution of Village Education Development Committees in the promotion of elementary education in terms of increase in enrollment, reduction in school drop-out rate and improvement in school result. Chapter eight presents the ground situation in terms of the conclusions emerging out from the empirical data and provides some of the recommendations for ensuring effectiveness of the Village Education Committees. A comprehensive bibliography is appended at the end of the Volume.

D.P. Singh
Ritu Mor

Acknowledgements

Community participation in school education through Village Educational Committees has been given utmost importance in most policy documents of the Government of India. As such, the new areas of research have been thrown open to the academics on various issues of community participation. The crucial link between community participation and equitable quality education has been the prime concern of the present study which aimed at evaluating the functioning of Village Education Development Committees in the state of Punjab. In successful completion of this elaborate Investigation, a number of individuals have contributed directly or indirectly in their own big and small ways. We indeed feel privileged to record our sincere appreciation and gratitude to each one of them.

To start with, we express our profound regards for Dr. Pushpinder Kaur for her valuable guidance and inspiring encouragement throughout the entire investigation. Her keen interest and enriching inputs on varied aspects of the principal theme helped the researchers develop a more critical and informed perspective of this issue.

We are whole-heartedly grateful to Dr. Meenakshi Sharma, Professor and Head, Department of Education and Community Services, Punjabi University, Patiala for her critical comments and useful suggestions at various stages of this work. Without her personal concern, it would have been rather difficult to have completed this Study in time. She was immensely gracious and forthcoming in giving her valuable time whenever we wanted to discuss anything on this Inquiry.

We express our sincere gratitude to all the personnel of the Sarva Shiksha Abhiyan and the Department of Education, Government of Punjab including the District and Block Education

Officers, Cluster and Block Resource Persons, Education Volunteers and the teachers for their valuable help, guidance and inhibited cooperation towards successful completion of this research study.

It gives us immense pleasure in acknowledging the help we received from the members of the Village Education Development Committees, the head teachers, the members of panchayats, the parent-teacher associations and other community people. It is needless to say that without their help, the Study would have been more open to criticism.

We would fail in our duty if we don't acknowledge our deep sense of gratitude to our son Arindam and daughter Arhana for depriving them of the love and personal attention and at times violating their right of protection from parental neglect. The patience exhibited by both these kids on the occasional neglect on our part has been phenomenal and we really appreciate their sacrifice once again.

We are indeed thankful to our friends Dr. Vasantha Rao from Hyderabad, Dr. Susant Panda from Pathankot and Dr. Sandeep Berwal from Sonepat for their unconditional and valuable academic inputs as and when requested. Finally, we take this opportunity to thank all our family members, near and dear ones, friends and colleagues for their genuine interest and continuous support for this endeavour.

D.P. Singh
Ritu Mor

CONTENTS

Preface v

Acknowledgements ix

Abbreviations xii

1. Community Participation: Meaning and Milestones 1
2. Decentralised Management of Schools: Some Important Government Initiatives 15
3. Voices from the Field: India and Across 24
4. Triumphs and Trails: Evidences from Some Selected States 57
5. The Manifesto of Participatory Management of Schools in Punjab 67
6. The Vehicles of Community Participation: Structure, Functions and Functionaries 86
7. Village Education Development Committees: Slithering towards the Sunshine 113
8. Witnessing the Present for Capturing the Future 158

Bibliography 177

Index 185

Abbreviations

BEO	Block Education Officer
BEP	Bihar Education Project
BRC	Block Resource Centre
CABE	Central Advisory Board of Education
CRC	Cluster Resource Centre
DEO	District Education Officer
DIET	District Institute of Education and Training
DISE	District Information System for Education
DPEP	District Primary Education Project
Ed. CIL	Educational Consultants India Limited
EFA	Education for All
EMIS	Educational Management Information System
GoI	Government of India
LJ	Lok Jumbish (Hindi Name of a School Education Programme)
MHRD	Ministry of Human Resource Development
MTA	Mother Teacher Association
MTC	Mother Teacher Councils
NCERT	National Council of Educational Research and Training
NCF	National Curriculum Framework
NCTE	National Council of Teacher Education
NGOs	Non Governmental Organisations
NIEPA	National Institute of Educational Planning and Administration
NPE	National Policy on Education
NUEPA	National University of Educational Planning and Administration
POA	Programme of Action
PRI	Panchayati Raj Institutions
PTA	Parent Teacher Association
SCERT	State Council of Educational Research and Training
SDMC	School Development and Management Committees
SIEMAT	State Institute of Educational Management and Training
SKP	Shiksha Karmi Programme(Hindi Name of a School Education Programme)
SMC	School Management Committees
SSA	Sarva Shiksha Abhiyan (Campaign for Education for All)
UEE	Universal Elementary Education
VEDC	Village Education Development Committee
VDC	Village Development Committee

1

Community Participation: Meaning and Milestones

Community participation for management of elementary education has been visualized as an important strategy in all policy initiatives at national as well as international levels. There is a worldwide consensus that for bringing the desired improvement in education, involvement of families and the community is inevitably important (Jomtien Declaration: 1990 and UNESCO Delhi Declaration: 1994). The policy-makers, practitioners, scholars, researchers, and communities around the world have been striving hard to attain the goals of universalisation of education through community involvement and as such participation of community in education has been acknowledged as the most crucial strategy in achieving these goals. The Declaration of the World Conference on Education for All, Jomtien (1990) and the UNESCO Delhi Declaration (1994) have provided a great deal of momentum to the community participation movement across the Globe.

Community participation in education in India is not a new concept. Community has always been thought as an integral part of the educational set up. Although the initially years of Post-independence India marked the centralization of education when the efficiency of the local bodies in applying their power properly was criticized (Wankhede and Sengupta: 2005) and a notion prevailed that everything belonged to the government and not the community, the idea could not sustain for long as centralization failed to affect a change in the quality of school education. (Noronha: 2003). The First Education Commission clearly spelt out the need of decentralization of school education and involvement of local bodies in the processes related to school improvement in 1966. According to the Commission, the immediate goal was to associate communities with the schools in their locality (GoI: 1966). Community participation as a primary strategy for ensuring decentralization in school education got another major boost with the adoption of National Policy on Education, 1986. The Policy laid primary emphasis on decentralized planning and management of elementary education in the country. The Policy visualized direct community involvement in the form of Village Education Committees (VECs) for management and improvement in school education at the village level. The Programme of Action (POA) 1992 further strengthened the Village Education Committees by providing that the State Government will lay down general guidelines regarding the constitution of village education committees and established norms of accountability in respect of the Heads of these institutions.

The 73rd and 74th constitutional amendments provided for decentralisation of the activities and facilitated the transfer of power and participation of the local self-government institutions or the Panchayati Raj Institutions (PRIs). Sarva Shiksha Abhiyan (SSA) assigned greatest importance to systematic mobilization of the community and creation of an effective system of decentralized decision making. The Right to Education Act 2009 also recognizes the role of local governance in school education by necessitating the formation of a School Management Committee (SMCs) in each school. Thus we see that community participation as a novel and unique approach, have always been emphasized in all the education related policy documents in India in order to build a synergic relationship between the community and the government with a view to create a sense of ownership and better resource management.

The present chapter deals with the general discussion on community participation in education while focusing on the need of conceptualizing and giving a very brief overview of the historical perspective particularly after India's Independence.

Conceptualizing Community Participation in Education

In reference to community participation in education, most stakeholders agree to the need to conceptualize the meaning of community, the nature of participation and the aspects to which participation is referred to including resource mobilization, management, monitoring, and evaluation, advocacy, and policy design (Noronha: 2003).

In education discourse, community has been defined in terms of parents, larger community and the elected representatives of the Panchayati Raj Institutions (PRIs) or the Village Education Committees (VECs) etc. Community, as such, can be viewed in two distinct perspectives. First, when community is taken to mean parents, then the background of children determines the caste-class composition, second, when the community is viewed as elected representatives, then their caste-class composition determines the involvement as well as the nature of conflicts arising out of that involvement. The caste-class composition in terms of socio-economic and educational background and status determines the role played by the community members and thus their involvement into various aspects of school education. The more spontaneous kind of involvement can be seen in terms of (a) parents being partners in their children's education by supporting them at home or (b) parents and community leaders showing interest in schools by contributing time or resources to support school development solve problems of space or facilities, lend a helping hand in school matters. (Noronha: 2003). Another dimension of community participation is political which often is viewed in terms of (a) playing a watchdog role-supervising and keeping an eye on the teacher (b) controlling the use of resources and their deployment; (c) raising issues of large educational change; or (d) influencing the curriculum and the way it is implemented. (Noronha: 2003).

According to Govinda (2003) community participation in education means the involvement of parents and community leaders as partners in supporting educational activities that contribute to improvement in their own lives. Shaeffor (1991) view community participation in primary education as any one or all of these viz., (a) the mere use of resources (such as primary health care facility); (b) participation through the contribution or extraction of resources (such as materials and labour); (c) participation through attendance (such as parents' meetings at school); (d) participation through consultations on particular issues;(e) involvement in the delivery of services; (f) involvement as implementers of the delegated powers; (g) participation in real decision making at every stage-identification of problems of, the study of feasibility, planning, implementation and evaluation.

In a broader sense, community participation refers to mutual collaboration, support and participation of families, community members and agencies, school staff, in the community or at school, in activities and efforts that directly and positively affect students' outcomes (Rani and Arora: 2004). In general, community participation in primary education means the involvement of parents and community as partners in supporting educational activities. Thus, community participation is a tool for self development and empowerment of community besides facilitating the achievement of the goal of universalisation of elementary education (Rani and Arora: 2004).

Govinda (2003) observes that community participation in the realm of primary education is a context-specific expression based on the degree of involvement of people, to bring certain systematic changes with a basic objective of ushering development and improvement in the quality of life of the participants, be it in the fields of health, education, social security etc. Further he has identified two categories of community participation in context of primary education as (a) exhorting community members to take active interest in the education of their children ;(b) liberalizing the administrative framework to make way for participation of community members in educational management.

The movement of community participation, however, has gone under a paradigm shift, in recent years, from a state of informal initiative to a formalized policy intervention. This can be witnessed from the documents and recommendations of various commissions appointed after Independence. There is a shift from non-participative administrative dominated educational planning to participative community-based procedure. This transformation in school education has gone through four important stages (Mohan, Devi Dutt, Antony: 2003).

1. The first stage consists of creating awareness among the parents about the importance of sending their children to school regularly. This assumes that persuasion, rather than enforcement or compulsion, is the means of ensuring universal participation of children in primary education.

This is evident from the legislative measures indicative of a shift from compulsion (as specified in the Compulsory Primary Education Act, 1961) to persuasion, combined with incentives to promote universal primary education as elaborated in various policy documents on Universal Elementary Education (UEE) and Education for All (EFA).

2. The second stage is characterized by increased awareness which, in turn, creates more demand for education. The government not being totally prepared to meet this increased demand, communities are invited to provide the schooling facilities in un-served areas. This intervention fulfills twin objectives of providing facilities to promote UEE and mobilizing community resources for education.
3. In the third stage, community support is sought and ensured while framing the provisions for establishing and managing new schools. This ensures not only participation, but also a sense of ownership as communities often provide the required space and other infrastructure facilities to run the school.
4. Sustainability of community participation is then to be ensured through the setting up of school betterment committees, which include members of the local community. These committees are primarily responsible for reviewing, organizing and mobilizing human, physical and financial support to better the functioning of schools.

Thus, community support, which begins as merely supplementary to the functioning of school, shifts emphasis to ownership of schools by community. Community participation thus gets integrated into the action plan for the goal of UEE. The constitution of Village Education Committees and vesting authority in them to oversee the functioning of primary school is one such example (Mohan, Devi Dutt, Antony: 2003). These committees are expected to develop into a participative system in which various stakeholders like the teachers, parents and community leaders work together with a common understanding to ensure maintenance of infrastructure as well as building an environment congenial to the teaching learning process.

The term 'community' for the purpose of present study refers to the village community in general and the Village Education Development Committees in particular. This way, community participation has been envisioned as the systematic involvement of the teachers, parents and other community members like the members of Parents Teachers Associations (PTAs), Mothers Teachers Associations (MTAs) and social activists (who, in turn, have been nominated to the Village Education Development Committees) in various aspects of school governance.

Communitisation of Elementary Education: The Milestones

Community participation in education in India has a long tradition. In the pre-colonial period, the education to the masses was available through *Pathshalas and Madrasas* which were managed by the local people. All the arrangements including procurement of teachers, contributing space to school and the facilities to students were made by the local communities. There used to be no central authority (like an education board) to design the curriculum but it was structured, though loosely, by the teachers and the community people together (Rani and Arora: 2004).

During the British period, the responsibility of organizing the school education was partially delegated to the Panchayats and municipalities. While the Government prepared the contents of education, the local bodies were responsible to organization and administration of the schools (Noronha: 2003).

In independent India, the universalisation of education was one of the constitutional prerogatives of the Government. This period marked the centralization of education. The government affected a takeover of the educational institutions as well as the cadre of teachers. The efficiency of the local bodies in applying their power properly was criticized (Mallik, 1996; Varghese, undated). The notion began to prevail that everything belonged to the government and not the community; therefore, it was the responsibility of the government to look after them. This notion, though, born out of an intention to improve the quality of education, could not sustain for long as centralization failed to affect a change in the quality of school education (Noronha: 2003).

The National Policy on Education (NPE) in 1986 envisaged a greater role for community in the field of education at the local level followed by various initiatives and programmes which indisputably underlined the importance of community participation in school governance. The successive governments made multi-pronged strategies entitling the community to be an active partner in the process of planning, implementation, monitoring and evaluating the school activities.

The following discussion would take us through various milestones in the journey for universalisation of elementary education in Independent India and the role of community as stressed and highlighted from time to time.

Based on the changes in the policies of the Central Government towards education, the educational development initiatives can be broadly divided into four different phases for easy understanding. The first phase can be from 1951 to the mid 1960s which is marked by expansion of formal education system to achieve universalisation of elementary education. The second phase could be from 1968 when first National Education Policy (NPE) was framed to 1986 when the second National Education Policy was framed. The third phase can be extended from 1986 to the 1992 when the NPE 1986 was revised followed by the initiation of the Programme of Action (PoA) 1992. The fourth phase can be understood to be from 1992 and onwards which is marked by the 73rd and 74th Amendments Acts, National Curriculum Framework 2005 and the Right to Education Act 2009 (Rao, V: 2008).

First Phase

Prior to India's Independence, the British established a system of education that had limited access and denied mass education. Macaulay explicitly stated that the objective of education system was to create a new breed of Indians as similar to the Europeans as possible. It was on account of this that the Indian National Movement developed a strong critique of the British system that only imparted 'learning skills' and not 'life skills' and that did not respect Indian traditions (Singh: 1999). Thus the National movement expressed the global sentiment of education for all. The imperatives of the colonial education policy prompted our leaders to search for alternative approaches to elementary education. Gandhi's approach of 'education for life', Rabindra Nath Tagore's approach of 'education for self-development' and Dr. Zakir Hussein's thrust on 'Nayee Taleem' formed the basis of future discourses on education. In the backdrop of Gandhi's emphasis on 'swawalamban' (self-reliance), the founding fathers of our Constitution recognized universalisation of elementary education as a crucial input for nation building. During this phase India has taken a pledge through the Constitution that free and compulsory education would be provided to all children upto 6-14 years of age. Article 41 and 45 of the Constitution provided the basis for the new approach. In the light of these articles, legislations for free and compulsory education were enacted and the children were exempted from tuition fee upto upper primary classes (Singh: 1999).

While Article 41 directed that the state shall, within the limits of its economic capacity and development, make effective provisions for securing the right to work, to education and to public assistance in cases of employment, old age, sickness and disablement and in cases of undeserved want; Article 45 directs that the state shall endeavour to provide, with in a period of ten years from commencement of this Constitution, for free and compulsory education for all children until they complete the age of 14 years. Article 21A, which was amended by 86th Constitutional Amendment Act 2002, provides that the state shall provide free and compulsory education for all children of the age of 6 to 14 years as the state may, by law determine. Article 21A also makes it mandatory that the schools will essentially be managed by School Management Committees (SMCs). Besides these articles, Article 24 and 39 also have the child in focus. Article 24 says" No child below the age of 14 years shall be employed to work in any factory or mine or engaged in hazardous employment" where as Article 39 says that" the state shall direct its policy towards securing that the tender age of children is not abused and that citizens are not forced by economic necessity to enter a vocation unsuited to their age or strength and that the children are given opportunities and facilities to develop in a healthy manner and in conditions of freedom and dignity and that childhood and youth are protected against exploitation and against moral and material abandonment. In the light of the Constitutional mandate of free and compulsory education, many states have passed legislations and provided facilities so that the children are able to go to school and the larger goal of universalisation of elementary education are fulfilled.

B.G. Kher Committee (1953)

Kher committee was appointed to examine the relationship between the state governments and local bodies in respect of the administration elementary education. The committee submitted its report in 1954 recommending that with regard to community participation and management, there is a need for decentralization to attract community involvement at the grassroots level. Thus all types of local bodies be involved to promote and manage education in the interest of mass education (GoI: 1954).

Balwant Rai Mehta Committee (1957)

Balwant Rai Mehta Committee submitted its report in 1957 suggesting that organization of Panchayati Raj (rule by village council) as an instrument of rural local self-government as well as an agency for community development. The major focus of the report was on democratic decentralization in all aspects of village development like health, education and development and so on. The Panchayati Raj has been designed to encourage the people of rural areas in meeting their needs locally. The committee recommended that primary education should become the responsibility of the Panchayats. In view of the recommendations of the committee, financial and administrative powers were transferred to Panchayati Raj bodies at the village level. Many states enacted Panchayati Raj Acts. Rajasthan was the first state to establish Panchayati Raj followed by Andhra Pradesh and Punjab (Rani and Arora:2004).

The first phase largely focused on the free and compulsory education of children so as to achieve the broader goal of Education for All (EFL) and Universalisation of Elementary Education (UEE). The recommendations of the B G Kher Committee, and Balwant Rai Mehta Committee were very significant development towards decentralization of primary education and involvement of community in the administration of school related activities.

Second Phase

The period after Independence saw a linear expansion of the elementary education but it was in 1964 that the Government recognized the need to take a holistic view of the education and thus appointed the National Education Commission (1964-66). The

Commission recommended a radical transformation in the prevailing education system and highlighted the need to promote equity and social justice. Following the recommendations of the Commission, the first National Policy of Education 1968 suggested for free and compulsory elementary education along with equalization of opportunities particularly to the vulnerable sections like the Scheduled Castes children and girls (Singh: 1999). This period also witnessed the decentralization of education where Ashok Mehta Committee (1978) strongly recommended for the transfer of powers to the local bodies for better participation of the community (Rao: 2008).

National Policy on Education 1968

National Policy of Education 1968 suggested for strenuous efforts for seeking free and compulsory education for all children upto 14 years. In respect of equalization of educational opportunities, the Pclicy stressed the need for more efforts and underlined that the regional imbalances in the provisions of educational facilities should be correlated and good educational facilities be provided in rural and other backward areas. The Policy recommended common school system to promote social cohesion and national integration. Common school system was essential to do away with the dual education system under which the children of the rich and well-to-do families avail education from private and good quality schools while the children from poorer households generally attended the public supported, free but poor quality schools. The Policy through common school system put emphasis on the proper integration of different bodies of school management like the government, local bodies and the voluntary organizations. However, inspite of far reaching recommendations, the Policy could not evolve a transformation of the education system that could relate more closely to the life of the people. The Policy was not even implemented by many states for the simple reason that education, at that time, was on the State List. Taking this fact into consideration, education was brought under Con-current List in 1976 through 42nd Constitutional Amendment Act (GoI, MHRD: 1986).

Ashok Mehta Committee (1978)

Ashok Mehta Committee formed in 1977 brought some new and significant thought in the concepts and practice of Panchayati Raj.

It re-emphasized the need for involving Panchayats in local development and planning and viewed their role in terms of strengthening the planning process at the micro level (Chaturvedi: 2003). Thus the Committee advocated transfer of substantial powers and responsibilities to Zilla Parishads. These included transfer of teachers, monthly transfer of salary funds and composition of a Board of Education for maintenance of the quality and standard of education (Rani and Arora: 2004). Under this Committee, district was made the first point of decentralization below the state level. The Zilla Parishad was made the executive body responsible for planning at the district level. However due to the collapse of the Janta Government before completion of its term, no action could be taken on the recommendations of the Ashok Mehta Committee report at the Central level (Rao: 2008).

Third Phase

The adoption of National Policy on Education 1986 was a significant development during this period. The Policy focused on the universal enrolment and retention of children upto 14 years of age and to bring a substantial improvement in the quality of school education. It stressed on community involvement in educational management as it would establish a close linkage between school and community and help in improving the quality of education, reduction in absenteeism, and irregularity. The Policy visualized direct involvement of community in the form of Village Education Committees.

The revised Policy on Education 1992 also emphasized for community participation in educational planning and management. After formation of the National Policy on Education 1986, a committee was set up under the chairmanship of Acharya Ramamurti in May 1990 to review NPE 1986. This Committee submitted its report in December 1990. Thereafter at the request of the Central Advisory Board of Education (CABE), another committee was set up under the chairmanship of Shri N. Janardhana Reddy to consider the modifications in NPE taking into consideration the report of the Acharya Ramamurti Committee. The Reddy committee submitted its report in 1992 which was broadly endorsed by CABE and adopted by the Government (GoI: 1998). The report of the Reddy's committee formed the basis of revision in the NPE 1986. The revised Policy 1992 assigned a major role to local communities through appropriate bodies to involve in the programmes of school management. The Policy laid stress on participation of non-governmental and voluntary efforts including social activist groups in planning, coordinating, monitoring and evaluation of activities related to educational development. The Policy keeping with the establishment of a participative educational order, strongly emphasized decentralization of educational management at all levels (GoI: 1998).

Fourth Phase

The most significant aspect of this phase was the implementation of Programme of Action (PoA) 1992. The reviews of NPE 1986 by the Acharya Ramamurti Committee (1990) and N. Janardhana Reddy Committee (1992) formed the basis for the Programme of Action (PoA) 1992.

Programme of Action (PoA) 1992

The National Policy on Education and PoA 1992 have emphasized the importance of decentralized planning and management of education at all levels and involving people in this process. The Plan of Action (1992) of the National Policy of Education (1986) said, "each Gram Panchayat may constitute a Village Education Committee (VEC), which would be responsible for administration of the delegated programmes in the field of education at the village level" (GoI: 1992). In pursuance of PoA, the Village Education Committees were formed as the structures for decentralized planning and management. The VECs have been entrusted with the responsibility to operationalize micro planning and school mapping in the village through systematic house to house survey and periodic discussion with parents. VECs were expected to build a congenial atmosphere through activities such as street plays, folksongs and rallies etc. (GoI: 1998). The PoA emphasized on reducing drop out rates, improving learning achievements and expanding access to students with community as equal partner in the educational process. Promoting parental and community involvement has been an essential aspect of school governance under NPE 1992 and the Programme of Action 1992 (GoI: 1998).

The 73rd and 74th Constitutional Amendment Acts 1992

The 73rd and 74th Constitutional Amendment Acts have provided for decentralization of powers and responsibilities to the Panchayati Raj Bodies. In pursuance of the provisions of the Acts, the state governments have taken steps towards devolution of powers to the PRIs with respect to educational governance and management. The 73rd Constitutional Amendment Act has identified 29 items for transfer to the Panchayats, including primary and secondary education. All states have enacted new Panchayati Raj Acts in order to realize the Constitutional mandate of decentralized democracy and development (Rao: 2008). The Acts fully acknowledge that the community is the main actor towards school governance and education related activities.

Sarva Shiksha Abhiyan (SSA) 2001

Community is the core actor in implementation of Sarva Shiksha Abhiyan. Community participation starts with the preparation of micro level planning at the beginning of every year. The Programme calls for community ownership of school based interventions through effective decentralization. The process is augmented through involvement of women's groups, village education committee members and the members of the Panchayat Raj Institutions. The issues relating to community participation under Sarva Shiksha Abhiyan are discussed ahead in a separate chapter.

The National Curriculum Framework (NCF) 2005

The National Curriculum Framework (NCF) 2005 is the principle document which provides a mean of evolving a national system of education. An important curriculum development principal was recommended by the National Policy on Education 1986 when it envisioned that "The National System of Education will be based on a national curriculum framework and would contain a common core along with other components that are flexible. The common core would include the history of India's freedom movement, the constitutional obligations and other content essential to nurture national identity. These elements will cut across subject areas and will be designed to promote values such as India's common heritage, egalitarianism, democracy and secularism, equality of sexes .... and inculcation of scientific temper" (GoI: 1986). The National Curriculum Framework (NCF) 2005 has emphasized strengthening of Panchayati Raj Institutions by adopting a more streamlined approach to encourage community participation as a means of enhancing quality and accountability. The Framework elaborates that the parents and community members could come into the school as resource persons to share their knowledge and experiences in relation to a particular topic being studied. The Framework clearly emphasized the role of community and parents' participation in overall development of children education. It said that participation of community in the child's world of education and learning should allow for the community to:

1. Transfer oral history like dealing with folklore and traditional knowledge like sowing, harvesting, monsoons, traditional crafts etc to children, while the school encourages critical reflection whenever it is required.
2. Support children in their exploration and creation of knowledge and information.
3. Support children in their practice of democracy through their participation in information generation, planning, monitoring and evaluation with local government and school.
4. Participate in setting criterion for vocational training.
5. Monitor the realization of children' rights as well as violations of these rights.
6. Enable the village to become a learning environment for children realizing the concept of the "village as a school".

The Document says that "community involvement can also be sought for maintaining the school and its facilities. There are examples of local contributions for building school boundary walls, augmenting facilities and so on. However, community participation must not mean the economic burdening of the poor families. On the other hand, there can be an understanding that school space can be shared with the community for local events and that there will be some collective responsibility in maintaining its premises" (GoI: 2005).

2

Decentralised Management of Schools: Some Important Government Initiatives

Community participation in school governance has always been central to achieving universal elementary education in India. Inclusion of minorities, women and socially deprived sections as stakeholders in the school education system has always been emphasized in major government schemes and programmes relating to school education. The present Chapter attempts to give a brief overview of some of the education related programmes implemented in different states by both the central as well as respective state governments for facilitating a congenial environment for participation of community people in the day to day governance of village school and which has been quite successful in making a niche toward democratic decentralization of school education.

Shiksha Karmi Project (SKP) 1987

Shiksha Karmi Project (SKP) was launched in Rajasthan in 1987 with financial assistance from SIDA (Swedish International Development Cooperation Agency). The project aimed at reaching out to children in remote and rural areas where the formal primary schools were either non-existent or dysfunctional. Under the Project local youth with some basic education were identified, trained and provided continuous educational support to teach children in Shiksha Karmi Day schools, Prehar Pathshalas (schools of convenient timings) and Angan Pathshalas (courtyard schools). (Ramachandran and Sethi: 2002). The concept of Shiksha Karmi was based on the assumption that a change agent, especially in the field of education, can work better if he/she belongs to the same locality. The involvement of the community in the identification of potential candidates and their recruitment as Shiksha Karmi was an important feature of the Shiksha

Karmi Project. A key element of the SKP was its emphasis on consensual functioning, with all decisions related to schools, selection of Shiksha Karmis, location of *Pathshalas* was to be taken in the Village Education Committee meetings (Ramachandran and Sethi: 2002). There was a great reliance on community support and each VEC consisted of members representing all castes, minority groups and women.

Total Literacy Campaigns 1988

Total Literacy Campaign and Post Literacy Campaigns were two flagship programmes of the National Literacy Mission Programme launched in 1988. Total Literacy Campaign has evolved along three basic principles. First, was to create a positive climate through mass mobilization and motivation, generating demand among non-literates for literacy and willingness among the educated to contribute and participate in the literacy campaign on voluntary basis. Second, was to design a cross-representative organizational structure and participatory management system which assured support of government and enable involvement of NGOs, voluntary agencies and all sections of civil society. Thirdly, the campaign gave stress on highly professional project implementation and management structure with inbuilt monitoring. Total Literacy Campaign was marked by massive environment building for mass mobilization, motivation and participation, a door to door survey to identify non-literates and other resources such as volunteer teachers and learners (CED: 2005). Total Literacy Campaigns were based on a unique social mobilization approach that involved all sections of the society from grass roots level to the highest level (GoI: 2010).

Bihar Education Project (BEP) 1991

Bihar Education Project represented the first major attempt in India to include a holistic approach to Education for All (EFA) using district as a basic unit of planning and implementation. The Project was conceived as a micro approach (village level) as well as a macro approach (state level) for universalisation of primary education. In the effective implementation of BEP, Village Education Committees played an important role (Planning Commission: 1994). Infact VECs were the fulcrum on which most activities of BEP revolved. VECs constituted women and members of disadvantaged groups, were instrumental in carrying out detailed micro planning exercise for building a proper environment for children' education. VECs played a positive role in raising people's contribution in construction and school improvement activities (Planning Commission: 1994). The VECs not only helped in micro planning but in many cases also acted watchdogs against the vested interests at the village level working against the BEP. Among major components of the BEP, one was to restructure the VECs to make them more effective and inclusive. The VECs formed before the implementation of BEP suffered from the basic problem that the members were being nominated by the Block Education Officer and the 'mukhiya' used to be made the president. During 1991-92, the BEP restructured the basic character of the VECs and the president now was to be directly elected by the Gram Sabha and the 'mukhiya' was not necessarily to be the President. The restructuring of VECs under BEP had a perceptible impact and there was a tremendous increase in enrollment after this restructuring (Kantha and Narain: 2002).

Rajasthan Lok Jumbhish 1992

Rajasthan Lok Jumbhish (meaning Peoples' Movement) project was launched as a people's movement at the grassroots level to mobilize support and participation of the rural community in primary education. The project was based on the assumption that the creation of a people's movement for primary education would generate a stimulus for human development which, in turn, would contribute to basic socio-economic change empowering the community as a whole (Govinda:1999). The core component of Lok Jumbhish was the participatory process of school mapping and micro planning. Under this, it was the villagers themselves who carried out the field surveys and prepared the education map of the village indicating the status of participation of every child. This approach indeed heightened the sense of commitment and accountability of the community members (Govinda: 1999). The Lok Jumbhish project broke grounds in Rajasthan by creating informal voluntary groups within the community in the form of a core team and a women's group in each village within the project area (Govinda: 2002). The Lok Jumbhish project empowered local people by involving them in school matters through carefully formed Village Education Committees making the participation more representative. Formation of a core groups and a women's group under Lok Jumbhish met the need for the coming together of people voluntarily for a common cause. It was the voluntary organization of the people that gave them a feeling of empowerment. In many villages core groups were transformed to VECs, thus, converting the informal organizations of the people into formal, legitimate structures (Govinda: 2002). The Lok Jumbhish project was able to transform, to a great extent, the centralized and hierarchical management systems of school education into people-friendly decentralized system in the state of Rajasthan.

District Primary Education Project (DPEP) 1993

District Primary Education Project has been one of the largest education projects of its kind in the whole world. The Programme aimed at achieving universalisation of elementary education in the country through district-specific planning with emphasis on decentralized management, participatory processes, empowerment and capacity building at all levels (Rao: 2008). DPEP stressed on the active role of the local community in promoting enrolment, retention, achievement and school effectiveness. The process was institutionalized through Village Education Committees and bodies like the Mother-Teacher Associations (MTAs). The VECs were entrusted with the responsibility of improving school facilities according to locally felt needs and priorities. The DPEP emphasized on local-specific planning in a participatory manner involving teachers, parents and Village Education Committees (GoI: 1997). To translate the idea of decentralization into an operational practice, the DPEP made following efforts (NIEPA: 1997).

1. The Programme identified district as the unit for initiating decentralized educational planning.
2. The Programme attempted to alter the pattern of resource decisions from state level to local levels.
3. The Programme attempted to strengthen the planning process to make it more consultative, participative and transparent.

The DPEP moved away from the schematic peace-meal approach of the earlier programmes and took a holistic view of primary education with emphasis on decentralized management, community mobilization and district-specific planning based on contextual and research based inputs (Rao:2008). At the village level, the implementation of the Project was monitored and supervised by the Village Education Committees, Mother-Teacher Associations, and Parents-Teacher Associations. The DPEP project was, however, not implemented in the state of Punjab.

Janshala Programme 1998

Janshala, which means community school, was a joint venture of the Government of India and the five UN agencies –UNDP, UNICEF, UNESCO, ILO and UNFPA to support the ongoing efforts of the Government towards Universalisation of Elementary Education. The approach of the programme was to promote educational planning and management through village based micro planning by local committees. Janshala was relatively a small programme in terms of its scope and coverage and the programme did not cover all aspects of primary education. This Programme aimed at:

1. Enhancing and sustaining community participation in effective school management;
2. Improving performance of teachers in the use of interactive child-centred and gender-sensitive methods of teaching and;
3. To redress social constraints with affect the attendance and performance of children, mainly the girls (GoI: 2002).

Janshala was implemented on the principle of decentralized planning and management. The Programme identified block as its operational unit rather than the district. Panchayati Raj Institutions were sought to play a more active role towards creating a congenial ambience for the decentralized planning giving greater voice to women, SCs/STs and the minorities (GoI: 2002). The VECs were actively involved in school improvement and other activities for universal enrolment and retention of children in primary and alternative schools. The Programme was implemented in the states of Andhra Pradesh, Madhya Pradesh, Maharashtra, Orissa, Rajasthan, Karnataka, Uttar Pradesh, Jharkhand and Chhattisgarh. The Programme completed its term in 2002, however, the term was extended till 2004 in some states. Janshala was the first programme in the world where five UN agencies collaborated and pooled resources to support an initiative in education (Planning Commission: 2007). The Programme amply demonstrated that flexibility and decentralized mode of functioning are pre-requisites for ensuring innovations at village, school and block levels (GoI: 2002).

Sarva Shiksha Abhiyan (SSA) 2001: Reaching the Unreached

The Sarva Shiksha Abhiyan (meaning People's Movement for Education to All) aims at universalizing elementary education by community – ownership of the school system. It is a response to the demand for quality basic education all over the country. The target beneficiaries in the community and other stakeholders are involved in all stages of implementation to achieve the education outcomes (GoI: 2000).

The Sarva Shiksha Abhiyan programme is also an attempt to provide an opportunity for improving human capabilities to all children, through provision of community-owned quality education in a mission mode. SSA assigns greatest importance to systematic mobilization of the community and creation of an effective system of decentralized decision making. SSA calls for community ownership of school-based interventions through effecting decentralization. Under SSA, concerted efforts have been made to mobilize the community to promote education, to help in development of educational facilities and to oversee the functioning of schools. It advocates for community based monitoring system with full transparency. Every school is expected to share all information with the community, including grants received. SSA envisages cooperation between teachers, parents and PRIs. One of the principal concerns in Sarva Shiksha Abhiyan is the education of girls, especially those belonging to the scheduled castes, schedule tribes and minorities. There is a focus on the inclusion and participation of children from SC/ST, minority groups, urban deprived children, children of other disadvantaged groups and children with special needs, in the educational process. On the whole, Sarva Shiksha Abhiyan is an effort to universalize elementary education by community-ownership of the school system through active involvement of Women's Groups, Village Education Committee (VEC) members, and members of Panchayati Raj Institutions. Overall Sarva Shiksha Abhiyan is understood in the following way:

1. A programme with a clear time frame for universal elementary education.
2. A response to the demand for quality basic education all over the country. An opportunity for promoting social justice through basic education.

3. An effort at effectively involving the Panchayati Raj Institutions, School Management Committees, Village and Urban Slum level Education Committees, Parent Teacher Associations, Mother Teacher Associations, Tribal Autonomous Councils and other grass root level structures in the management of elementary schools.
4. An expression of political will for universal elementary education across the country.
5. A partnership of the Centre, State and the local government.
6. An opportunity for States to develop their own vision of elementary education (GoI: 2000).

Broad Strategies Central to Sarva Shiksha Abhiyan Programme (SSA)

Institutional Reforms: As part of the Sarva Shiksha Abhiyan, the Central and the State governments undertake reforms in order to improve efficiency of the delivery system. The States will have to make an objective assessment of their prevalent education system include in educational administration, achievement levels in schools, financial issue; decentralization and community ownership, review of State Education Act, rationalization of teacher deployment and recruitment of teachers, monitoring and evaluation, status of education of girls, SC/ST and disadvantaged groups, policy regarding private schools and Early Childhood Care and Education (ECCE). Many states have already carried out several changes to improve the deliver system for elementary education.

Sustainable Financing: The Sarva Shiksha Abhiyan is based on the premise the financing of elementary education interventions has to be sustainable. This calls for long-term perspective on financial partnership between the Central and the State governments.

Community Ownership: The programme calls for community ownership of school based interventions through effective decentralization. This will be augmented by involvement of women's groups, VEC members and members of Panchayati Raj institutions.

Institutional Capacity Building: The Sarva Shiksha Abhiyan conceives a major capacity building role for national, state and district level institutions like NIEPA/NCERT/NCTE/SCERT/SIEMAT/DIET. Improvement in quality requires a sustainable support system of resource persons and institutions.

Improving Mainstream Educational Administration: It calls for improvement of mainstream educational administration by institutional development, infusion of new approaches and by adoption of cost effective and efficient methods.

Community Based Monitoring with Full Transparency: The Programme will have a community based monitoring system. The Educational Management Information System (EMIS) will correlate school level data with community-based information from micro-planning and surveys. Besides this, every school will be encouraged to share all information with the community, including grants received. A notice board would be put up in every school for this purpose.

Habitation as a Unit of Planning: The Sarva Shiksha Abhiyan works on a community based approach to planning with habitation as a unit of planning. Habitation plans will be the basis for formulating district plans.

Accountability to Community: Sarva Shiksha Abhiyan envisages cooperation between teachers, parents and Panchayat Raj Institutions, as well as accountability and transparency to the community.

Priority to Education of Girls: Education of girls, especially those belonging to the scheduled castes, scheduled tribes and minorities, will be one of' the principal concerns in Sarva Shiksha Abhiyan.

Focus on Special Groups: There will be a focus on the inclusion and participation of children from SC/ST, minority groups, urban deprived children, children of other disadvantaged groups and children with special needs in the educational process.

Pre-Project Phase: Sarva Shiksha Abhiyan will commence throughout the country with a well-planned pre-project phase that provides for a large number of interventions for capacity development to improve the delivery and monitoring system. These include provision for household surveys, community-based micro-planning and school mapping, training of community leaders, school level activities, support for setting up information system, office equipment, diagnostic studies, etc.

Thrust on Quality: Sarva Shiksha Abhiyan lays a special thrust on making education at the elementary level useful and relevant for children by improving the curriculum, child-centered activities and effective teaching learning strategies

Role of teachers: Sarva Shiksha Abhiyan recognizes the critical and central role of teachers and advocates a focus on their development needs. Setting up of Block Resource Centres/Cluster Resource Centres, recruitment of qualified teachers, opportunities for teacher development through participation in curriculum-related material development, focus on classroom process and exposure visits for teachers are all designed to develop the human resource among teachers.

District Elementary Education Plans: As per the Sarva Shiksha Abhiyan framework, each district will prepare a District Elementary Education Plan reflecting all the investments being made and required in the elementary education sector, with a holistic and convergent approach. There will be a Perspective Plan that will give a framework of activities over a longer time frame to achieve UEE. There will also be an Annual Work Plan and Budget that will list the prioritized activities to be carried out in that year. The Perspective Plan will also be a dynamic document subject to constant improvement in the course of programme implementation (GoI: 2000).

The Right to Education Act 2009

The Right to Education Act 2009 is another historic step which recognizes the role of local governance in school education. The Act specifies that a School Management Committee (SMC) shall be constituted for every school to monitor and oversee its working, and to plan and facilitate its overall development with representation of parents, teachers and community and local authority members, as may be prescribed by the appropriate State government. The SMC shall exercise such powers and perform such functions, and shall be accountable in such manner, as may be prescribed. The composition of the School Management Committee shall be so prescribed that: i) It has adequate representation of all sections of the community, including parents, teachers, scheduled castes, scheduled tribes, other backward classes, and persons/bodies working for education, and ii) At least half of its members are parents/guardians of children studying in the school. The Act further underlines that all moneys received by a School Management Committee for the discharge of its functions under this Act, shall be kept in a separate account, and shall be utilized in such a manner as may be prescribed by the respective state government. And the accounts of money received and spent by the SMC shall be maintained and audited in such manner as may be prescribed.

3

Voices from the Field: India and Across

Community participation in education in India has always been thought as an integral part of the educational set up. Since the First Education Commission in 1966, the need of decentralization of school education and involvement of local bodies in the processes related to school improvement have been clearly spelt out. Thereafter, in 1986, community participation as a primary strategy for ensuring decentralization in school education got a major boost with the adoption of National Policy on Education. The NPE 1986 visualized direct community involvement in the form of Village Education Committees (VECs) for management of elementary education. The Policy viewed Village Education Committees as bodies that could ensure participation of every child in every family in primary education either formally or through non-formal means. Immediately after that the Programme of Action (POA) 1992 further strengthened the Village Education Committees by providing that the State Government will lay down general guidelines regarding the constitution of village education committees and establish norms of accountability in respect of the Heads of these institutions. The major responsibility of the village education committee was to operationalise micro level planning and school mapping in the village through a systematic house to house survey and discussions with the parents. The 73rd and 74th Constitutional Amendments in 1992 also provided a fillip for decentralisation activities and facilitated the transfer of power and participation of the local self-government institutions or the Panchayati Raj Institutions (PRIs). The PRIs have also, been delegated responsibilities with regard to location and relocation of existing primary and upper schools on the basis of micro planning and school mapping. Under these Acts, decentralization of school management to grassroots level bodies was an important policy initiative. District Primary Education Programme (DPEP) one of the most comprehensive programmes launched in 1994 with international assistance from World Bank and European Union was designed primarily as a decentralized program to address local needs and circumstances by involving local stakeholders. The communities were required to establish Village Education Committees (VECs) under DPEP. Local groups including Parent Teacher Associations (PTA) and Mother Teacher Councils (MTC) were also encouraged to participate in VECs. The Lok Jumbish (LJ) and Shiksha Karmi Programmes (SKP) launched in 1994 stressed on mobilizing the village community to take responsibility to universalise and deliver quality education. The positive impact of the LJ and SKP served as a model for designing innovative approaches for community involvement in all educational activities of a village school in the country.

Sarva Shiksha Abhiyan (SSA) launched in the year 2002, aimed to Universalize Elementary Education (UEE) through people's involvement and participation. SSA assigns greatest importance to systematic mobilization of the community and creation of an effective system of decentralized decision making. It calls for community ownership of school-based interventions through effecting decentralization. It puts a great deal of emphasis on the civil society for ensuring the effectiveness and viability of our school education. Institutions such as Village Education Committee/School Management and Development Committee/ Ward Education Committees have been set up at village or school level in almost all the states to ensure community participation in the school education system. The Right to Education Act 2009 is another historic step which recognizes the role of local governance in school education. The Act specifies that a School Management Committee (SMC) shall be constituted for every school to monitor and oversee its working, and to plan and facilitate its overall development with representation of parents, teachers and community and local authority members, as may be prescribed by the appropriate State government.

In the light of the preceding scenario, community participation in school education has emerged as a new area of research for the academics. But so far very limited efforts have been made to evaluate the functioning of Village Educational Committees which are the primary institutions for facilitating people participation at the grass roots level. Some studies on the working of these committees have, though, been carried out in some states in India as also in other countries but the issue calls for a more comprehensive and proactive approach. Some of the studies conducted are being presented here.

Menon (1996) in her study to operationalize participatory decentralized model of development with community initiative in a rural society of Mewat region of Haryana underlined the need to search for all possibilities so that the people are made primary agent of their own development through education and organization. The researcher is of the view that development at grassroots level cannot achieved without the participation of the community. The Village Education Committees (VECs) play a vital role in the improvement of enrolment of children specially girls. These committees were active in ensuring retention and in reducing the drop-out rate. The study highlighted that the VECs emerged as effective instruments for people's involvement in the school management. Due to the proactive role of these bodies in this region, the rate of enrollment of girls increased from 7.37 per cent to 37 per cent and similarly for boys the enrollment increased from 44 per cent to 88 per cent. The writing and instructional materials provided by these institutions were received well and properly utilized by the students. The door to door canvassing by the VECs to improve the enrollment was very effective.

Lal (1997) in his study on "Community participation through Village Education Committee (VEC) in primary education in selected blocks of Sitamari district in Bihar" found out that VECs in this district were constituted through general meetings of the village with active participation of the school headmaster and village leaders. There was no proper representation of women, scheduled castes and scheduled tribes and minorities. The participation of district BEP officials and Block Education officer (BEO) was very poor in the process of formation of VECs. The members were mostly middle aged upper caste, educated, agriculturists. The awareness level about their role and functions, however, was below average. Monthly VEC meetings were held regularly on a fixed date in the school campus. There was no coordination between VEC and *Mahila Samooh* in the village. There was a general lack of interest among members and there was lack of coordination between community, school and government functionaries. Appropriate block level structures (Cluster Resource Centre) were in the process of being created so as to collaborate in the activities at the intermediate level between the village and the district. On the whole, majority of the VECs were not doing well in this state.

Menon (1999) in her on "Functioning of Village Education Committees (VECs): A study of selected VECs in Haryana" found that in Haryana, the role of VECs is yet to establish a link between the school and the community. Nevertheless a significant number of members of VECs had educational level up to the secondary stage and above. The composition of the VEC in this state ensures 50 per cent representation for women. However, the participation of women is limited in terms of the actual role in the functioning of VEC is concerned. The women still observed *purdah* and many of them do not even look up to male members and speak. This reticence and non-participation of women effect the functioning of the VECs as many of the local issues remain unaddressed. In some cases, however, the woman *pradhan,* who is usually an elderly woman, was more vocal. The emergence of sub-districts structures like the Block Resource Centre while envisaged as a professional support mechanism has created some problems in the existing educational administration framework. There is apparently some conflict about the roles. The role of Village Education Committees has been predominantly in areas related to accessibility and participation of children, particularly girls. Enrolment in the first three classes has increased considerably though the teacher-pupil ratio stands as 1:70. Enrolment of girls has been perceptibly high in areas where girls' school has opened. There is a visible change in the attitudes towards girls' education. The grants made available through DPEP for innovative projects and preparation of low cost teaching material has been utilized to the maximum. The Village Construction Committee (VCC) has emerged as a very vibrant structure activity involved in improving the school and its surroundings.

Kumar et al. (1999) studied the community participation in primary education and school effectiveness in the city of Baroda. The study found out that the schools under Baroda Municipal Corporation (BMC) don't form Parents-Teachers Associations whereas other schools had formed PTAs. The members of the PTAs usually participated in the celebrations of national days, sports days and result declaration day. In some cases the PTAs even sponsored few activities of the school like school magazines, sports etc. This study also underlined that there is a positive relationship between the community participation and the school effectiveness which means that greater the community participation greater is the school effectiveness. In the sampled schools a significant number of voluntary organizations (176 out of the total 504) participated in the school governance activities in the city of Baroda.

Tyagi (1999) studied Village Education Committees in Ranchi District and found that inspite of the VECs under the Bihar Education Project, there are a number of issues which need to be addressed and looked into for strengthening the educational planning and management structure at the village level. To ensure that the right persons are elected to the VECs is a great difficulty since the influential and powerful people want to see themselves or their favourites as VEC members. The study revealed that nearly half (4 to 5 members each) were not attending the meetings regularly and not taking part in any school activities. They did not even know the specific objectives of these bodies. No efforts were being made by anyone to ensure that good people come to these committees who work with interest and devotion. The study further shows that *mukhiya* of the panchayat is not necessarily the right choice for presidentship of VEC. There was neither any formal mechanism for decision making nor there was any process for feed back to the VECs. This lackadaisical approach leads to frustrations among members dampening their initiative and sapping voluntary spirit. Members demanded that the venue of the meetings should be *tola-wise* so that general public and the people belonging to particular *tola* can also attend the meeting. One of the main difficulties which VECs face in performing their functions was that they didn't have any financial and administrative powers.

Ed. CIL. (2000) in its report based on a study conducted on community mobilization and empowerment for universalisation of primary education in selected states of India underlined that in order to enhance community mobilization and participation in primary education different contextual strategies and methods as per the local culture and traditional folk through institutionalized structures like the NGOs, BRCs, CRCs and PRIs proved very useful. The media campaigns in addition to special programmes on radio, production of audio cassettes, printing of newsletters etc. undertaken for mobilization as well as promoting intensive participation of the community greatly impact the micro planning process at the village level. The teachers and community members trained for this purpose took up micro-planning activities such as social and resource mapping, identification of out of school children, development of a village education register, village education plan etc. The report brings forth that the VECs, as such, have envisaged as a key institutions for community mobilization, participation and empowerment under DPEP. Almost all the states focused on sensitizing the VEC member on primary education and in states like Karnataka and UP, training were conducted through participatory techniques. Training modules have been developed on majority of states through resource institutions such as DIETs as well as with the help of NGOs and resource groups formed at the district level. The study showed that there was satisfactory participation of VEC members including woman at VEC meetings, however, the articulation of women at these meetings was limited by the presence of male members. While in Himachal Pradesh there was an awareness about DPEP amongst the Panchayat Raj Institutions (PRIs) representatives, in other states such as Assam, there was little interface and this required reinforcement. In Bihar there was virtually no interface as the Panchayat Raj system was non-existent. In states such as Himachal Pradesh, Bihar and Uttar Pradesh, NGOs were involved with community based strategies in the field. A few sampled states had organized training of teachers in community participation. In Assam, all the teachers interviewed for the study had undergone training with a module on community participation and the role of VECs. In Gujarat, nearly 50 per cent of the teachers had received this training; in Uttar Pradesh, more than half of the head teachers were imparted a 10 days training in the DIETs of the district concerned.

Narayana and Chandrakant (2000) studied the functioning of VEC in Satra district in Maharashtra and underlined that the co-ordination between the VEC and the higher authority like Block Level Education Authority or District level Education Authority was very less. The conduct of the meetings also needed improvement. In this district, it was observed that no proper notice was given by the Secretary of VEC to the members about the schedule of meeting. There was no proper representation of female and people belonging to reserved category. The educational authorities had done little with regard to proper monitoring and mentoring the VEC meetings. No or very little attention was being paid towards conducting any training programmes for the VEC members.

Sujatha and Rao (2000) conducted a study on "Community Participation in Education in Tribal Areas: Study of Maabadies (community schools) in Vishakhapatnam District of Andhra Pradesh". They found that the VECs in this area had been clearly involved in planning and implementation of educational intervention and conduct atleast one meeting in a month. Interestingly more than 80 per cent heads of the household, even those who were not VEC members, attended the VEC meetings. There were cases where the VEC collected money from the community and paid salary to the teachers from the community funds. In about three-fourth (70%) of the villages, new school buildings were also constructed by the community either by providing manpower or material or money. Mothers' Committees were also constituted in some villages to help the VEC in the management and preparation of Mid-Day Meal Scheme. The study establishes that, on the whole, the VEC in this area functioned satisfactorily.

Bhattacharya (2001) in the study on functioning of village education committees in selected VECs in Ghunucha cluster of Morigaon district of Assam found that all the sample VECs were constituted within the Government guidelines. All the VECs under study were formed in public meetings arranged by CRC Co-coordinators or the Head teachers of primary schools of the villages. The composition of VECs was uniform and complied with the Government rules. The minimum qualification of president of VEC was fixed at matriculation and as a result, more than two-fifth (40%) VEC Presidents were replaced by qualified persons in the year 2000. Interestingly more than two-third of the total representatives of VECs were from Mothers' Committees. The mothers' committees appeared to be very active in the entire sample VECs and more than half (50%) mothers units were fully involved in school as well as village development work. Nearly 70 per cent VECs were found to be active whereas in case of 30 per cent VECs, the working was not satisfied. However the VEC members along with the teachers prepared the action plan in most of the VECs.

Mathew (2001) conducted a study on community participation in the development of primary education in Kerala and found that the vicious circle of poverty compelled the poor parents not to participate in a satisfactory way in the school activities. The role of Panchayat Raj institutions with regard to monitoring has been significantly apprehended by the teaching community. The role of PRIs, in initiating quality improvement drives and cultural networking in the village, has remained far from satisfactory and there was a significant vacuum with regard to an integrated institutional mechanism at the panchayat level, which takes care of both the infrastructural as well as qualitative needs of the school. The different committees functioned as rather independent entities, with little or no give and take. On the other hand there were no clear policies on primary education in the state, which swing the panchayats into action. The teaching community in Kerala obviously needs proper monitoring even as a few teachers had demonstrated excellent examples of meritorious work in this state.

Nayak (2002) conducted a study on "Role of Village Education Committees (VECs) at Primary School Level in Cuttack District of Orissa" and found that a great majority of the members of VEC in Cuttack district don't attend the meetings of VEC regularly. There was no orientation among the members about the role and responsibilities of these committees. Only 54.16 per cent of VEC members were visiting their school regularly and making efforts at their level to ensure the regular attendance of children in the schools. A little more than half (52.08%) of the VEC members were of the opinion that there was a visible impact of their interaction with parents on student' enrolment. Even then a great majority of these members did not approach the parents and convince them to send their children to school. According to Nayak only 45.83 per cent of VEC members did sincere efforts to understand and empathize with the needs of the girl children.

Ed. CIL (2002) in its study on "role of family, community and school factors in improving retention and achievement level of disadvantaged children" underlines that training imparted to VEC members motivate them to help in enhancing enrolment and retention of disadvantaged children in their respective schools. In the area of the study training of VEC members increased the parent teacher interaction and about 94 per cent parents started visiting the schools. 63 per cent parents reported to have had a good relationship with teachers. The study further highlighted that most of the parents held the view that the education is not seen to be a useful preposition as long as the employability of the children is not assured. Nevertheless many parents regarded education as valuable but their poverty kept their children away from school.

The increase in dropout rate of children as per most of these parents was due to poverty and involvement of children in domestic work. It was rather unfortunate that the upper caste teachers did not like to have meetings with lower class parents. Many parents in the areas of the study wanted introduction of vocational education at lower level of schooling so that education proves useful to their children. Provision of mid-day meals, scholarships and free text books had played a vital role in increasing enrolment and retention of disadvantaged children but their achievement level still remained poor. Poor teacher–pupil ratio was a big problem for children. Although there was improvement in infrastructural facilities and school atmosphere but still much more was to be done. Use of Teaching Learning Material (TLM) had attracted children of disadvantaged community to a great extent. According to the study DPEP has greatly changed the attitude of the people about education.

Government of Karnataka (2004) in collaboration with Azim Premji Foundation studied School Development and Management Committees (SDMC) in Karnataka. The study found out that 2 per cent of the schools in Karnataka didn't even have a School Development and Management Committee. The monitoring mechanism seemed to be ineffective. There was low representation of girls as student representatives in SDMCs. 68 per cent of the student representatives who were interviewed were boys only. Action is required to encourage girl students to take part in the SDMC activities. Students from SC/ST communities also need representation since they are still an underprivileged section. The significant findings of the study were that as against the general perception that Presidents of SDMCs were illiterate, it was found that 90 per cent of them were literate. During the field study, it was observed that illiterate members were as effective as literate members and educational qualifications, therefore, could not serve as a basis for selection of the members.

Vaijayanti (2005) examined various aspects of involving the community in elementary education with particular reference to the role of School Development and Monitoring Committee SMDCs) in Karnataka. The major scope of the study was to know the a) general facilities available in the village to ensure universalisation of Elementary Education; b) Level of awareness of the members about the various aspects of the SDMC and their socio-economic status and their degree of participation in school;

c) to know the availability of information about SDMCs and d) Procedure and process adopted for their formation; and the perception of government functionaries on the functioning of SDMCs. The study was carried out across 469 schools and over 4,500 stakeholders in eight districts of Karnataka were interviewed. The major recommendations of the Study are following:

1. SDMCs should be continued and their autonomy protected by insulating them against political interference -both in their formation and day-to-day functioning.
2. There is ambiguity and confusion in the prevailing Government circular on the formation of SDMCs. Modifications suggested while retaining the content and spirit of the first executive order.
3. Involve SDMC members with reasonable qualifications (SSLC and above) in curriculum construction, teacher training and other academic issues; a register be maintained to record the visits and the suggestions made by members.
4. Encourage all schools to maintain a list of alumni to collect contributions from them for the corpus fund. The list to be prepared in consultation with SDMC members.
5. Create a platform to share 'Best Practices' among the SDMCs at cluster level and arrange exposure visits for the members to schools where SDMCs are functioning effectively.
6. Arrange periodic meetings by SDMC presidents in a block/ cluster to share their experience. And Sabha/Gram Panchayat meetings should discuss school issues.

Kumar (2005) studied community participation in primary schools of Municipal Corporation of Delhi. The study found out that the parents' interaction with the teachers in sampled schools was not adequate due to lack of time with them. Teachers in these schools were of the view that the parents render help in organizing the school functions but they help teachers in monitoring attendance of the students only occasionally. There is Parents-Teachers Associations (PTA) in the schools but they don't work satisfactorily. The PTA meetings are conducted in a routine manner rather than focusing on the problems of the schools and the students. With regard to the views of the head teachers, the study underlines that the parents take initiatives in getting admissions of their children but many of the parents don't find enough time to get feedback about performance of their children on a regular basis. About one-third of the head teachers expressed that the parents come to them with complaints about the teachers mainly relating to not taking classes regularly, not checking or giving homework. Parents don't provide any guidance services to the children relating to information on job and fulfillment of children' needs. So far as the opinion of the parents is concerned, more than half of them expressed that they contact the head teachers and teachers to know about the education of their children. Almost of the parents said that they help and assist their children in their studies as per the suggestions of the teachers. Kumar has emphasized in his study about the importance of community participation in academic aspects like increasing attendance, reducing school drop out and improving school results. Participation of the parents is also important in financial aspects like generating funds, sponsoring awards, prizes and functions of the school. Community can help the school in construction of buildings, boundary wall, toilets and other civil works.

Wankhede and Sengupta (2005) in their study of the Village Education Committees in West Bengal found that the VEC members in all the studied schools were involved in ensuring regularity and punctuality of attendance of the teachers, ascertaining use of the pedagogical methods taught in the training and looking after the level of learning of students. Other aspects, which VEC members in various schools claimed to supervise, included sitting arrangements of students and the condition of school buildings and attendance of students at school. However, their frequency of visiting the school for the purpose of such supervision varied significantly. Teachers in all the four schools said the majority of the VEC members visited school only when a VEC meeting was called. Whatever the form of such supervision was, the school teachers seemed to welcome it. Analysis of the process of VEC formation makes it clear that there is no scope for the poorly educated people to be part of VEC. However unethical it may sound, probably it would not be desirable also to nominate such people as the decision-makers for issues related with education. However, they should be given the scope to voice their opinions, i.e., they should be empowered in case they are socio-economically disadvantaged. The study found that unstable economic capacity of people was often behind their poor participation in public works and dropout of their children from school. Therefore, one step towards empowering socio-economically disadvantaged population would be betterment of their economic strength. In this regard, gram panchayat may play a vital role through employment generation schemes as well as through poverty alleviation programmes. Significant amount of resources have already been spent in this regard. However, the majority of the efforts have been wasted due to improper vision and unplanned implementation. What is required is developing planning capacity at gram panchayat level. For this, regular and effective training programmes are essential. Only localized planning can make it possible to contextualize a governmental programme to the needs of the local community. Another way of empowering the local community would be by bringing vibrancy in various public fora. One such forum relevant for this context is meetings between VEC functionaries, school teachers and the parents/guardians. A similar forum for discussing broader developmental issues is the meeting of gram sangsad. It is necessary to make common people more responsive and vocal in these meetings. This can happen only through reconstruction of local power structures.

Yadav (2006) in his study on role and performance of VECs in Haryana suggested that only those members should be nominated who are at least matriculate and there must be a fixed tenure for each member. It should be made mandatory for all members to attend the meetings. Community leaders should extend full cooperation to VECs for better functioning of the schools. In his study he found out that there was no sharing of the responsibility among the VEC members while only four VECs have made contribution towards construction of classrooms and drinking water facilities. There was no coordination and rapport between Parent Teachers Association and the VEC although there were two representatives of PTA in each VEC.

Banerjee et al. (2007) report the findings of a survey in a rural district in Uttar Pradesh. Rural households, parents, teachers and VEC members were surveyed on the status of education services and the extent of community participation in the public delivery of education services. Most parents do not know that a VEC exists, public participation in improving education is negligible, and large numbers of children in the villages have not acquired basic competencies of reading, writing, and arithmetic. The authors are of the opinion that in order to stimulate an active participation of village people in improving education, direct steps should be taken. It cannot be presumed that the mere presence of a VEC can create a basis for community-based activism that would substantially transform the educational scenario in these villages. It is therefore, natural to ask whether some form of the village-based campaign that informs people about the provisions, resources and the existence of the VEC and the roles it might play, can stimulate participation and activism to the point where it begins to affect the state of education in the village.

Govinda, R. and Diwan, Rashmi (2007) in their book on community participation and empowerment in primary education presents the grassroots experiences, problems encountered, and lessons learnt from community participation initiatives launched in five Indian states of India namely Madhya Pradesh, Karnataka, Rajasthan, Bihar and Kerala. The contributors shed light on how decentralization in education has been actualized in different parts of the country and cover a wide range of important issues including how community participation works in an environment characterized by deep-rooted socio-economic divisions; the equitable distribution of participation; identifying and defining the community; and ensuring the genuine representation of those who are traditionally excluded from decision-making in rural areas. The experiences provide valuable insights in finding ways to bring about genuine partnerships between civil society, the administration and NGOs in the drive to achieve universal education. The book stresses the point that community participation can play an important role in promoting primary education. In India, decentralization has been identified in recent years as an essential component of the process of educational reforms and change. Decentralization has resulted in many efforts to bring community and school close together as also to involve community members in the development of primary education programmes.

Sinha, Sujit (2007) while sharing the experiments of the NGO – Swanirvar in North of 24 Parganas in West Bengal on community participation in primary schools reiterates that encouraging parents to come to school during school hours and watch what their children were doing proved very useful. Parents were asked to maintain individual records of the children. The teachers made home visits, mainly to households where the children were "weak" or faced some problem. This strategy was quite worthwhile and over a period of time the drop out rate in schools reduced and enrollment also started showing improvement. According to Sinha, community participation is very important in school management and VEC or Village Education Committee need to be given more and more powers. Swanirvar tried to involve the community people in (a) physical and material contribution, and (b) decision making, planning, monitoring and control type of activities. Apart from that the parents were also involved in the participatory evaluation of the school and the teachers and also in making the Teaching Learning Material. The parents were broken into 4 to 7 groups depending upon the number present, and asked to formulate, after discussion among themselves, their opinion on three aspects of our schools. Then they had to make a presentation on (a) what things they liked about our schools; (b) what things they did not like there and would like to change; and (c) what new things they would like to see. The study highlights the participation was wonderful and in order to ensure even a more better community participation in school governance, there is a need to reorient the bureaucrats, the state decision makers in matters of syllabus and text books, members of the inspectorate, the teachers' training institutes, and the existing teachers. Participation of local NGOs in this aspect can prove very beneficial.

Mor (2008) in his article 'encourage community participation' underlined that the school-community partnership in education gives a right to the parents to choose the kind of education that their children should get. It can achieve many objectives, including increasing the relevance and quality of education, improving ownerships, reaching disadvantaged groups, mobilising additional resources and building institutional capacity. In Punjab, for managing the school affairs, the community in the form of panchayat, parent-teacher association and village education development committee (VEDC) has been empowered to inspect schools, monitor the academic performance of children, attendance and quality of education, supervise regular supply of quality and hygienic mid-day meals, supervise and monitor aspects relating to distribution of textbooks, maintenance and repair of building, creation of infrastructure at the school and community levels, ensuring drinking water and toilets, ensuring cleanliness and sanitation, ensuring the proper utilisation of grants, participation in micro-planning process and organising community mobilisation activities for developing better coordination between various stakeholders. The VEDCs, which are particularly made for supervising the quality of elementary education, have been formed in almost all the villages. These bodies usually consist of seven-eight members, including Scheduled Castes and women members. The study conducted by the author in Moga and Ferozepur districts of Punjab found that in Ferozepur district, stresses that issues relating to elementary education were not even discussed in more than three-fourth gram sabhas. Quality issues have no place in VEDCs meetings. A great majority of VEDCs/ PTAs and gram sabhas don't have education on their priority list. In Moga, the proportion of gram sabha not discussing elementary education issues was as high as 90 per cent. Those VEDCs, which discussed something on education, took up only those issues that involved money, e.g., construction of building, toilets, and the repair of boundary wall. Sadly enough, more than one-fourth VEDCs members did not even attend the meetings. Those who attended were emphatic in saying that they attended the meetings just to complete formality and had no interest in quality issue of elementary education. Parents, who can afford, don't even prefer to send their children to government-run schools. Majority of such parents were simply indifferent to the kind of education being imparted in government schools.

Pandey, P. *et al.* (2008) evaluates the impact of a community-based randomized controlled trial to determine the impact of information dissemination on learning and other school outcomes. The information campaign gave information to the community, village education committees and parent teacher associations on their oversight roles in school management as well as the services they are entitled to. The hypothesis was that school outcomes may improve if the community has detailed information about the control it has over the schools and the services parents are entitled to from the school. The study was conducted in three Indian states, Karnataka, Madhya Pradesh (MP) and Uttar Pradesh (UP). Even though all three states have devolved oversight roles to the community, they differ in the extent of oversight devolved. In Madhya Pradesh, *a* Parent Teacher Association (PTA) is mandatory in every school and parents of all children enrolled in the school are members. The PTA has an executive committee which runs the PTA, though all parents are supposed to participate in decision making. The school headmaster is the secretary of the PTA and a parent is the chair. The executive committee has 14 members who elect the PTA chair from among them. The PTA chair and the head teacher jointly operate the school account. The school account receives annual grants for repair and maintenance, for school development, teaching learning material (TLM), money for school dress, money for civil works – school building, rooms, toilet, drinking water etc and money for mid day meal. Every school in Karnataka has a mandatory School Development and Monitoring Committee (SDMC). The SDMC members include the head teacher of the primary school, elected members of the village government and parents of children. One of the parents is the chair of SDMC. SDMC chair and the head teacher jointly operate the school account. The SDMC can inspect the schools and complain to the district or block education office. In Uttar Pradesh, a village education committee (VEC) is mandatory in every *gram panchayat*. There is one VEC for all the primary and junior government schools in the *panchayat*. The VEC typically has 5 members – it is headed by the *gram pradhan* (who is the elected head of the village government). Other members include the senior most head teacher among the schools, and three parents of children in these schools. The *pradhan* and the head teacher jointly operate the school account. The study highlights that a large proportion of the committee members in all three states stated not having received any training from the government regarding their roles and responsibilities. Parent members of these committees had the lowest positive responses. About 20 per cent of parent members reported receiving any training in Karnataka, compared to 8 per cent in MP and 2 per cent in UP. In all of the states, headmasters seem to be most informed about the roles and responsibilities of the school committee. Parent members of the committees seem to be the least informed and participating the least, particularly in MP and UP. Parent members of the school committees in Karnataka seem to be more informed about their roles and report somewhat greater participation in meetings and school inspections as compared to MP and UP.

Shankar Girija, K. (2008) in his article on 'Community Involvement in Sarva Shiksha Abhiyan: An Assessment of the

Village Education Committees in India' brings forth that the Village Education Committee has the most significant role to play in implementing of Sarva Shiksha Abhiyan at the grassroots level. The author has suggested that in order to make the involvement of VECs in school management and administration more effective, it is recommended that (i) every year, the VEC members should be given training on mode of operation of VEC meetings, role and responsibilities of VECs, facilities and grants available under SSA and MDM and monitoring of school activities; (ii) The CRCCs and BRCCs should interact with the VEC members more frequently and motivate them to participate in school management and development more effectively; (iii) Each District Project Office of SSA programme should classify the VECs in to different grades basing upon the extent of their participation in school management and development; (iv) the low grade VECs should be given more attention for activation; (v) In order to motivate the VECs to take part more effectively in SSA activities, rewards may be given to some selected VECs who have shown exemplary performance and (vi) VECs may be encouraged to take up innovative measures to achieve SSA goals at school level. VECs should be repeatedly guided in conducting micro planning exercise for their schools.

Dash and Panda (2009) carried out a study on the effectiveness of Village Education Committee on promoting universal elementary education in Nabarangpur district of Orissa. The effective VECs of different areas were selected by purposive sampling. For the present study, 30 VEC members were selected and were interviewed by developing a structured interview schedule. The authors highlighted that most of the Village Education Committees worked excellently well for all round development of primary schools. All the VECs took care and management work of primary schools satisfactorily. VECs organized different awareness programmes satisfactorily for attitudinal change of villagers. Facilitation role of all VECs were very impressive. VECs undertook different steps to improve the financial status of primary schools. Proper care and management of primary schools, taking steps to increase enrolment and to reduce drop-out rate, organizing different cultural activities in schools, working for development of school environment and helping the teacher to prepare TLM were significant works of VEC, which significantly affected the environment of the local primary schools. Facilitation role, attitudinal role, school improvement role, economic activities and miscellaneous works have been performed by VECs effectively for all round development of the respective school. The study concluded that the role of VECs is very essential and important for the improvement of primary education. The success stories of different VECs would certainly act as examples for the weaker VECs so as to improve working style for improvement of management system and effective participation. Since Nabarangpur is a tribal dominated district, it will be helpful for other tribal school VECs to learn to bring change in their mode of activities for all round development of primary school in respect to enrolment, retention, achievement and school environment etc. The authors emphasized that the function of community is proved to be very effective in all kinds of activities in the school like care and management, enrolment, teaching learning processes, organizing different cultural activities, maintaining a clean school environment, preparation of TLM and sustenance of financial support to the school.

Government of Maharashtra (2009) Department of School Education and Sport in its *Annual Work Plan and Budget Document* 2009-10 for *Mid-day Meal (MDM) in Schools* have fully authorized the Village Education Committees (VECs) to implement the scheme at school level. Funds are provided to the VECs and they have been given full powers to expand the scope of their working so as to improve the school education in the State. They have been empowered to inspect schools, maintenance and repair of building, creation of infrastructure at the school and community levels, monitoring the academic performance and attendance of children, supervising and monitoring the distribution of textbooks, ensuring drinking water and toilets, ensuring cleanliness and sanitation, ensuring the proper utilization of grants and participation in all micro-planning processes. The Government of Maharashtra, in the *Annual Work Plan and Budget Document* 2009-10, has decided that the mid day meal scheme is to be implemented by the VECs at village level, by the Ward Education Committees (WECs) at the Municipal Corporation or the urban level and the School Management Committees (SMCs) to be responsible in the Private-Aided Schools. The VECs, WECs and the SMCs have been authorized to appoint agencies like Self Help Groups, *Mahila Mandal,* needy women or NGOs for full involvement of the community particularly at various levels. Since the scheme has been totally decentralized, the community participation has increased tremendously in the state and this model has worked very well so far. Mother's involvement in supervision of cooked meals has helped children to participate in the school activities more actively.

Nayak, P.M. (2009) in his book on Community Participation in the Universalisation of Primary Education emphasizes that people's direct participation in the management of primary education is felt indispensable and inevitable for materializing long cherished goal of universalisation of primary education. Specific efforts in various forms have been launched to revitalize the school-community relationships that can be gainfully channelized for quantitative as well as qualitative improvement of primary education in the country. This book is based on a study of eight villages across two districts of Orissa and focuses on the role of the community in planning, management and organization of school activities. It explores the actual and expected roles of the School Management Committees (SMCs) in school governance. A total of 160 respondents were drawn on the basis of purposive sampling across 64 SMCs in the State. The study found that the working of the SMCs was not at all satisfactory. The meetings are either not held at all or, if held, they are just once in a year. One-third respondents stated that the SMC members did not attend the SMC meetings whenever they are held. Various problems perceived as impediments in the working of the SMCs were inadequacy of teachers, poverty of members, lack of sufficient financial aids, lack of coordination among members, inadequacy of classrooms, lack of incentives for SMC members, political interference and reservation of SMC seats in the village community. Interestingly gender of the chairman of SMC was perceived to be important for the effective functioning of these bodies. The men argued that they are better in governing the SMC than their women counterparts. The study further underlined that caste, class; gender and political affiliation of members do affect the functioning of the SMC in multiple ways.

Rao, Vasanta Srinivasa (2009) in his study evaluated the working of the school education management committee (SEMC) in a tribal area of East Godavari district of Andhra Pradesh. The respondents for the study were members of the SEMCs. Among the three categories in each SEMC, two parents out of four, one member of the Panchayati Raj Institution (PRI) either panchayat president or panchayat ward member whoever was available – and all schoolteachers/headmasters (in the study area most of the schools were single teacher schools or with a maximum of two teachers) were covered. 125 respondents were selected by simple random sampling from 26 SEMCs in 26 sampled villages of the three mandals. The study found that that community participation in improving education is negligible and that members of the school education management committees have limited awareness of the Sarva Shiksha Abhiyan (SSA). The study indicated that more than 67 per cent of all categories of the respondents were aware of SSA. An overwhelming majority (87.2%) of the schoolteachers were aware of SSA, whereas in the case of PRI members it was 61 per cent and among parents of the school-going children, the percentage was 52 per cent. The SEMC members (17%) suggested that creating awareness among the tribal parents would enable them to participate in school related activities. The other suggestions were to introduce mid-day meal programme on a daily basis in the schools, making drinking water available in the premises, use of TLM materials by teachers, provision of better infrastructure schools and so on. All these suggestions reveal that the tribal community members were participating in some way or the other in school-related activities. These community level structures i.e. SEMCs play a key role in micro-planning, especially in the development of a village education plan and school improvement plans.

Institute of Rural Research and Development (2010) in its report on capacity-building needs of Village Education Committee in villages of District Mewat, State of Haryana explored the effectiveness of the VECs in influencing the access to and quality of education in 13 villages of this district. It investigated the level of knowledge and awareness of VEC members pertaining to their roles and responsibilities, and about Government policies and constitutional rights for the promotion of formal education. Furthermore, it also explored the level of involvement of members in education related activities in villages and coordination among VEC members, schools and District administration. The findings revealed that the effectiveness of VECs in the villages is limited. More than half of the VEC members are inadequately informed about their roles and responsibilities. Their participation in activities to ensure quality formal education in the villages is also inadequate. The members admitted to having received no formal training, before being made members of VEC. The involvement of VEC members in activities as stipulated in VEC guidelines is negligible, and even VEC meetings are not organized on a regular basis. The members are not involved in budget tracking and many of them are not aware of annual funds granted to VECs. Effective engagement of VEC members with the community is missing in almost all villages. Across villages, the level of knowledge and participation of members varies. It has also been observed that the literate members of the VEC are usually more informed and involved. Similarly, male members are more aware and participative, as compared with female members. The report suggests that there is need to build the capacity of VEC members around their entitlements and responsibilities. Such a capacity-building program must aim to educate the members about importance of VEC, reason behind the formulation of VEC and its role in ensuring quality formal education in villages. The program must also ensure that the knowledge gained by VEC members gets translated into affirmative action by members at village level.

Zingkhai and Asung (2011) in their article published in the *Sangai Express* bring out the dismal state of affairs of Village Education Committee in the state of Manipur. According to the authors, in 2011 alone, in the month of April, these bodies were known as VEC (Village Education Committee) chaired by the Headman, in the month of May, they were named as SMDC (School Management and Development Committee) chaired by the Headmaster, and in the month of June, the name was further changed to SMC (School Management Committee) chaired by the District Councillor. Highlighting the misadventures in governance of the Government of the State of Manipur, the authors laments that the composition and nomenclature and its frequent changes of the village level education committees in the hills, is more surprising and interesting. The trajectory of the three different types of nomenclature and composition of the committees in just three months does not show these bodies in a good light. The first Committee which was known as VEC, till 15th April, 2011, had the Headman/Chief as the ex-officio Chairman. The second Committee that short lived for less than two months was known as the SMDC with Headmaster (or the senior most teachers in the absence of Headmaster) as the ex-officio Chairman. The third Committee which is the latest is known as the School Management Committee (SMC) as per vide order NO.30/19/09 –SE(S), Secretariat: Education Department (School Section), dated the 14th June, 2011, which says that the Member of District Council of the area in which the school is located shall be the Chairman/Chairperson of the School Management Committee (SMC). The Headmaster (or senior most teacher in absence of Headmaster) shall be the Member Secretary. The Bank account of the Committee shall be operated jointly by the Headmaster and Executive Director of DRDA concerned. As per the opinion of the authors the District Councillors instead of strengthening the efficiency of village level committees, have an implicit intention of institutionalizing a covert ploy to loot the money granted, which in the end, would also loot the 'Right of Children to Free and Compulsory Education' asserts the authors.

Aikara J (2011) studied the decentralization of elementary education and community participation in Kerala. There are two structures for decentralization of elementary education. One is the representatives of the local self government while the other is in form of representatives of civil society organizations. In the process of decentralization in school education all state schools in the state are brought under local self governments. Involvement of civil society is a form of both decentralization and community participation. Participation of the local self government is the result of the direct dispersion of power from the State government whereas the civil society participation in elementary education can be considered as the result of 'deemed to be decentralization' in so far as the state recognizes and/or supports the efforts of the representatives of civil society organizations in providing elementary education. According to the author although there is decentralization in the form of state systems and state-civil society partnerships, the major aspects of school education are with the centralized state department of education. The local self government and the civil society elements function for certain aspects of elementary education that are decentralized from the state central authority. The main function decentralized to them is the provision and maintenance of infrastructure of the school under their jurisdiction. Decentralization of education in Kerala has not resulted in greater participation of the stakeholders like teachers and parents in school management. The author has stressed that for decentralization to lead to greater community participation, there is a need for more convergence of state support and the social capital of the civil society.

Experiences from Across the Borders

Haq (1996) examines the status of community participation and the factors which may contribute to the more active participation of community in primary education in Bangladesh. Data for the study were collected through personal interviews and focused group discussions with parents, teachers, local opinion leaders and government officers involved in school management. The study selected a sample of 180 parents, 36 community leaders, 36 school level implementers (Head Teachers, SMC/PTA members and Taluka Education Officers) from six districts of Bangladesh. The main sampling unit selected was the school. The 18 primary schools were selected on the basis of their geographic and residential (urban/rural) location. The study indicated that the nationalisation process of primary schools did detach the community from a sense of ownership of their local school. Most schools rely very little on their local managing bodies (SMC and PTAs) which play a symbolic rather a powerful and active voice for their school. Parents and guardians identified that they were the key people to keep contact and make the link between the school and community. It appeared from the discussion of the focus groups of SMC and PTA members that the community has a feeling of moral obligation to the school and that people were willing to donate things to the school as well as look after school property while teachers are away. Parents reported that they were willing to take care of school, if asked, to enhance it's upkeep and appearance. Study concluded that the local people at all levels are still interested in schools and are ready to contribute in the form of management and supervision provided government is willing to acknowledge their contribution. It was recommended that wider level community participation could be enhanced by a wide range of socio-cultural activities and sports.

Rashid and Salam (1999) studied two Village Development Committees (VDCs) in villages Pahankucha and Gudaraia of Bangladesh with particular reference to the country's development programme named as Watson programme. The aim of this programme was to have safe water, hygienic latrines and overall hygiene practices in the rural community. Apart from that the programmes also aimed at making people aware of the benefits of sending their children to school, plantation, clean environment, various income generating activities and drawbacks of the dowry system and women oppression. According to the authors, the aim and goals of the Watson programme cannot be attained by ensuring the participation of only a particular sector of the community. The spontaneous participation of the targeted community as a whole is a pre-requisite for the successful implementation of the development programme. All classes and sectors of the community should be organized and their active participation should be ensured. This is why community approach instead of target group approach is proved to be more effective in successful implementation of Watsan programme. The key functions of the VDC are to make adjustment between the existing problems and resources by taking necessary decisions. The VDC sometimes acquires resources from outside in order to solve the village problems. Thus it ensures the happy atmosphere and an overall development of the village. The study found out that the VDC members are very enthusiastic about the work they have been doing, their successes, and the issues they plan to tackle in the future. They are proud of the achievements they have made in the safe water and sanitation department, in the remarkably short time. The VDCs are ready to throw themselves wholeheartedly in the attempt to make the people realize the need for safe water, hygienic latrines and overall hygiene practices. They talk to the villagers, and visit all the houses. Their success is due to the fact that they make people realize the need for development. The VDC has performed a remarkable role in raising the use of hygienic latrines in the village. The VDC has conducted different programmes such as courtyard meeting, discussion in the mosques, and has encouraged the rural people through interpersonal communication to construct and use hygienic latrines. The VDC has been successful in carrying out its motivational programmes due to its system of communicating through the local opinion leaders such as Imams (Religious leader of the Muslim community), school teachers, and local government members. Moreover, they are encouraging people not only on hygienic latrine and safe water use, but also making them aware of the benefits of sending their children to school, plantation, clean environment, various income generating activities and drawbacks of the dowry system and women oppression.

Eldah et al. (2004) explored community schools in Kenya and role of community in funding and managing these schools. In Kenya community schools in Kenya are defined as schools which are built, financed and managed by the communities themselves, with or without government assistance. The authors have emphasized that the community schools play an important role in providing alternative channels for students enrolled in non-formal education to join the formal education system. The present study was confined to a sample of nine schools in Nairobi province and in Rift Valley province – Kajiado district. These schools were selected on the basis of their different features in view of representing the various types of schools offering primary and secondary education in Kenya. The study revealed that these schools are constantly expanding their contribution to the achievement of the goal of basic education for all in the country, despite the many challenges facing them. Dropout rates in these were low. Some of these schools offered lunch to students, which helped to keep them in school. The majority of teachers were poorly paid but they remained in the job because of their commitment to the learners and their parents. They needed better supervision from the government and opportunities to upgrade their levels of competency. Infrastructure facilities needed to be improved and land ownership is a potential source of conflict between the schools and the churches which very often own the land where schools are built. The study points out that there is a need for the Kenyan Ministry of Education to assist these schools to cope with their main problems in the areas of teachers' salaries, pedagogical improvement, and supervisory services. Although the community schools do not always abide by policies, norms, regulations and standards established within the legal education framework, it is important for the government to acknowledge the role that these schools play in increasing access to and participation in primary education to many marginalized groups. The government, within the free education policy framework, is duty bound not only to maintain the quality of education offered in the community schools, but also to support the schools (both government and community initiated schools) through the provision of teaching-learning materials, teacher training, school feeding, pre-service and in-service training of teachers, and meeting part of the teachers' and non-teaching staff salaries. It is incumbent on the government to develop sustainability measures to ensure continuity of the programmes after donor withdrawal in many of the community schools.

Tom-Miura, Allison (2004) in her Doctoral Dissertation, University of Southern California, Los Angeles on "Engaging Communities in the Planning of New Urban Public Schools" examines how school districts and communities can work together to address facility and academic achievement inequalities affecting African-American and Latino students, as part of their school construction programs. This study explores the hypothesis that when school districts engage community stakeholders in a clear, consistent and meaningful way in the long-range planning and site selection of new public schools, they can build schools more effectively and achieve better academic outcomes and overall benefits for impacted communities, as well as increased support. A case study of the Los Angeles Unified School District (LAUSD) sheds light on the numerous challenges school districts face in engaging communities as key partners in the long-range planning and site selection process for new urban schools while trying to address educational and facility inequalities and community development needs. From 1999 to 2001 quantitative and qualitative data on LAUSD was collected through first-hand observation and from primary and secondary sources. Qualitative research on the community engagement practices and policies of thirteen other school districts from nine different states was collected through the use of surveys and phone interviews. Promising practices were identified from these school districts, chosen for their high rates of growth and active school construction programs and key guiding principles were developed. The research provided invaluable insight on how school districts can more effectively engage communities in the long-range planning, prioritization, and site selection process for new urban schools while working to reduce facility and educational inequalities and support community revitalization and development needs.

Beyene, Y. et al. (2005) conducted a study on "stimulating community participation in primary schools" to know a) why does community participation in Ethiopian schools need to be stimulated?; b) how does community participation impact school quality? and c) what are the characteristics of a community that make its members more willing to participate in schools? The findings of this study underlined that the community participation projects must properly account for the local context in order to adequately address the barriers to quality education. Because the setting in which schools are found is so important, different approaches must be utilized in rural and urban areas. Urban areas are more likely to be overloaded with competing demands by various developmental actors and may have priorities that are vastly different from governmental directives. In contrast, rural areas are generally much more receptive to outside intervention, principally because they have been given less attention historically. The research found that greater attention must be placed on the role of women in the program. Women are not as actively involved in PTA committees as men and as such, are much less likely to contribute to financial decision-making. They are, however, having profound effects on female enrollment through their involvement and activities within the Girls' Advisory Committees. Last, the lack of knowledge sharing among various implementing partners is being addressed by USAID, but efforts to increase collaboration are still in their beginning stages. The study expressed that the Basic Education Strategic Objective Program II (BESO II) could be strengthened by helping communities to diversify the forms of participation, taking greater care to understand the local context and barriers to change, being aware of the unintended (and potentially negative) consequences of their efforts to promote greater community involvement in schools, insisting upon planning for the future, and incorporating more flexible approaches to curricular design and scheduling in the formal education sector to ensure sustained community participation and high enrollment rates in primary education. Study believed that the community participation had a positive impact on the quality of education in Ethiopia. Most of the community members wanted to get involved in the school activities and were stimulated and mobilized.

Hill, F. (2005) in his article on "Community Involvement – Is It Rinky-dink or a Chance to Think?" underlined that community involvement as part of the facility planning process has been around for a long time. Today's parents are more informed, success-oriented, and technology savvy than ever before. They know what they are doing at work, and are demanding that the skills and knowledge necessary for success will be available to their children. For effective involvement of parents in school activities the teacher should adopt a more personal approach. The author reiterates that in the American context, the teachers must identify successful students (present and past) and their parents along with their phone numbers. Then the teachers must personally call and alert the parents to the upcoming request for them to attend a facility planning meeting or other such activity in the school. After that, the teachers should follow up with a "personal note" – which means a personally signed note, addressed specifically to the parents. (Not a mass mailer). Then, make a reminder call prior to the meeting to confirm time, location, and agenda. According to Hill, these and other such strategies for community involvement definitely produce good ideas, improve community support, and make the process worthwhile. They have worked well all across America.

USAID (2005) started a programme for Community Participation for Improving Schools with the collaboration from World Education in Mali in Sub-Saharan Africa to assist the community in conducting a community education assessment. As an experiment, the programme was first launched in Bambougouwere, a small village in Mali. In this village many children were being kept out of school, particularly girls, because they were needed to help out with chores at home, and because the school was so little valued. The programme helped the community to identify and prioritize their educational needs, and examine cultural and social practices that influence their children's educational opportunities. This program aimed at enhancing community participation in schooling thus mobilized, the Parent Teacher Association (PTA) which then began changing the face of education in Bambougouwere. The PTA constructed three new classrooms. They repaired the roof to the school using locally donated materials and funds, and they furnished the classrooms with enough dried mud benches for all students. More than that, the PTA mobilized groups of parents to talk to other parents to reduce the amount of work children do at home, so that they are free to attend school and study. The PTA brought their concerns not only to the local office of the Ministry of Education, but also to the town's mayor. As a result, the school has two new, better qualified teachers, and the mayor's office is supplying the school with chalk, notebooks, and a new well so that children will have potable water. Enrollment in the school increased. Bambougouwere is just one of 405 public schools that USAID supports in Mali to improve the quality of education for over 16,750 students.

Bobekova, Elvira (2007) in her paper 'Decentralization of Education in Rural Kyrgyzstan' sets out to understand the decentralization process in the post-Soviet Kyrgyz Republic with special attention to rural schools and their communities' capacity to sustain them under decentralized management. The ideas about the hindrances to educational decentralization in rural Kyrgyz Republic derive from the author's field research. The collapse of the Soviet Union (USSR) in 1991 had a tremendous disruptive impact on the economic and social institutional structures of the Kyrgyz Republic. Despite the sound basis of universal literacy developed by the USSR under a centralized education system, the new independent state pursued educational reforms, the primary feature of which was decentralization. The push for decentralization came from the shift to a market economy that made it difficult for the Government of the Kyrgyz Republic to finance education. A decentralized approach to education was seen as the path to development for a country striving to build a democratic society. Decentralization was also seen as a way to relieve the financial burden of running schools and improve the quality of school education. The Government of the Kyrgyz Republic shifted partial financial responsibility for schools to local governments and delegated some autonomy to schools, assuming that decentralization would increase the participation and accountability of key school actors, attract local resources, and improve the quality of education. Decentralization is largely seen by the Government of the Kyrgyz Republic as a cost saving policy, but the reality is that the center must provide the required expertise and financial flow in order to sustain and nurture its successful implementation. Much of the success of decentralization depends on the parents' and local actors' attitudes, actions, and performance. Therefore, information is an essential part of the successful implementation of decentralization. Parents and school administrators need to be given relevant information, at least about simple indicators of relative performance such as preparation of teachers, spending per child, and educational outcomes. Decentralization does not guarantee efficiency. This is only developed through experience. Accountability cannot simply come into being. It needs to be nurtured. Decentralization is a complex process that involves actors and institutions outside the schools. Therefore, any reform to the education system requires a holistic approach. Currently in the Kyrgyz Republic, decentralization is rhetorical. The reasons for this are much more complicated than stated here, because it is not a linear process and it involves a number of interconnected institutions.

Parajuli, Mahesh Nath (2007) in his study on People's Participation in School Governance in Nepal found that each studied village had a School management Committee (SMC). But in many cases people, particularly women and low caste, did not know its existence. People are not much informed about who runs or manages the school or they think that teachers run or mange the school. Even those who have heard about the SMC, many did not know their expected roles. Most people think that their expected role is to provide labour contribution to school or just sending their children to school. People did not know about the financial situation of the school nor were they aware whether they have a right about enquiring about the financial situation. They think that they did not have such right. The study underlines that people's knowledge of and participation in school management helps understanding their response to the state initiatives of decentralization regarding school governance. People's knowledge is very important and successful in management of school. In Nepal schools were effectively governed by the community until 1971, when they were nationalized and placed under the central state. Later the Nepali state started to translate the hegemonic international targets and elements from the world models into the national and then the local programmes – Decentralization and local involvement. The Nepali state has repeatedly claimed that decentralization has led to people's participation in the governance of the school at the local level. However, the state policy is to seek decentralization and participation according to the state's agenda and not in accordance with people's agenda. Analyzing people's knowledge about and participation in decentralization and school governance and making a critical assessment of state policies in this regard, it is found that the state policies and practices do not promote participation of local people in the governance of the school in their locality. At the district level it is shown that the district planning process is very much committed to transforming the national programmes or fulfilling the national targets and least concerned with the context at the district or at the local level. Hence the process has remained a centralized practice. The study concludes that centrally managed structures and hierarchical social structures and practices are some of the factors that prohibit people's participation and keep them away from village social processes. Due to these reasons the village schools were unable to make a place for themselves in village social space.

The International City/County Management Association (2008) in its special edition IQ Report brings forth that the community-oriented schools in US are generally more sustainable because these schools encourage broad community involvement in school facility planning and provide high-quality education. They are relatively smaller size and have the capacity to fit gracefully into the neighbourhoods they serve. They are located within a neighbourhood and are safe for children to walk or bike to. They act as a neighbourhood anchor and support community use of the school facility after school hours. These schools enhance teaching and learning, and accommodate the needs of all learners and result from a planning and design process involving all stakeholders. The schools provide health, safety and security and make effective use of all available resources and allow for flexibility and adaptability to changing needs of the students and community members. Community-oriented schools have tremendous impact on the communities in terms of community cohesion, social equity and quality of education. In many cities and towns, these schools serve as community anchors that support greater community interaction, engagement, and pride. The socioeconomic makeup of neighbourhoods is reflected in a community's schools, and has important implications for academic equity. Academic success, teacher satisfaction, parental involvement, attendance rates, graduation rates, and student safety are greatly influenced by school size and use, including the degree to which it is integrated into broader community life.

UNICEF (2011) in its report on 'Schools of Quality: The Lao Approach to Child-Friendly Schools' examines the Schools of Quality (SoQ) Programme of the Lao People's Democratic Republic. As per UNICEF, SoQ is the rights-based, child-friendly approach to improving the quality of education in the country. The SoQ approach aims to ensure all children realize their right to a basic education of good quality that prepares them with the life skills required to be healthy, productive members of society, prepared to face the challenges of a fast-changing world. Schools of Quality work closely with communities to ensure that all children enroll attend school regularly and complete their primary education. All stakeholders are involved in developing and maintaining a healthy, safe, supportive and protective environment for students and teachers, including provision of clean water supplies and an adequate number of toilet facilities for girls and boys. The SoQ actively encourages community members to participate in school development as well as teaching and learning. A close working relationship is maintained with the community, primarily through the Village Education Development Committee (VEDC), to ensure universal enrolment and support for quality teaching and learning. Teachers communicate with parents in support of their child's learning. The school director provides leadership and support for teachers and students and takes a lead role in promoting education in the community. The VEDC provides guidance in school planning and management activities, ensuring the school improvement plan is implemented. Communities in the Lao People's Democratic Republic have a long history of supporting schooling through financial or in-kind contributions. They typically provide village land for the school, construct or assist in construction of school buildings, offer accommodations and food supplies to teachers, and in some cases, recruit community members to serve as teachers when no government-provided teachers are available. The SoQ approach is transforming community interaction with schools in fundamental ways. Child-seeking activities, for example, have raised awareness of community obligations to ensure access to education for all children and have encouraged joint responsibility for creating conditions that enable this to be achieved. Community members are engaged in a sophisticated assessment of their school against the SoQ dimensions and standards, using the indicators as a guide, and become more aware of what quality schooling should look like. For many, it represents the first time they have discussed education with school staff in such detail. Throughout the lengthy process, staff and community members grapple with concepts and their application to the realities of their lives. Because the self-assessment requires consensus, it builds common understanding of the state of their school – identifying aspects in which it excels, aspects in which it lags behind expectations and priorities for improvement. The report reiterates that the SoQ program has been very successful in improving the standard of education in the Lao People's Democratic Republic.

Summing Up

It is evident from the foregoing discussion that although community participation in the processes of educational change and reform has been acknowledged as very important the world over but the results so far are still far below the expected standards. While there are numerous success stories, the failures remain far too many. Community participation in school governance as a people movement still remains a distant dream. The experiences have shown that socio-economic and cultural constraints like ignorance, illiteracy, poverty, patriarchy and gender-based stereotypes of the community members continue to act as impeding factors towards achieving a more inclusive and equitable school education. The experiences in many Indian states reveal that in rural areas many parents do not even know what a Village Education Committee (VEC) is all about. The monitoring mechanisms for the bodies made for ensuring community participation like the VECs, PTAs, MTAs and PRIs; continue to remain ineffective, by and large. The lack of coordination and rapport between various stakeholders like the teachers, parents and Panchayati Raj functionaries is another factor that weakens the working of these community-based institutions. Mere presence of a VEC in a village is less likely to transform the educational scenario so long as the members of these committees are not active and sensitized. It is important to understand what the expectations are and perception of the people about the whole process and what mechanisms and strategies should be used to make them more effective. The present volume underlines the importance and pertinence for finding out some effective ways and means for strengthening the village education committees and consequently making these bodies more functional and efficient.

4

Triumphs and Trails: Evidences from Some Selected States

Participatory school governance has been the core of all policy documents related to school education in the country particularly after the National Educational Policy 1968. The Village Education Committees (VECs) have been visualized as effective instruments for ensuring not only community participation but also improving quality as well as governance of the school at the village level. In many states where the community people have been pro-active and vigilant, VECs have played a vital role in reducing school dropout rates and improving enrollment of children in village schools. These bodies have done an impressive work in improving the overall teaching learning environment both within and outside the class rooms. However, in many states, the performance of these bodies has been far from satisfactory. The VECs in such states have drastically failed in meeting their pre-determined goals. The VECs exist only on papers. No meetings are held. The parents didn't even know about the existence of a VEC in their village. A great majority of gram sabhas don't have education on their priority list. In nutshell, the VECs are yet to show the expected results towards achieving universalisation of elementary education through community participation. Some experiences are being presented from selected states in India depicting the success stories as well as the failures of the village education committees in the following section.

Experiences from Bihar

In Bihar, the VEC is also called the Vidyalaya Shiksha Samiti (VSS) and is comprised of 15 members, out which, nine members are the parents while three are non-parents elected by the local community. Two non-elected community members are nominated by village

Mukhiya. Of the twelve elected members of the VEC, there has to be at least five female members. One male and one female member each from scheduled caste, scheduled tribes and other backward classes are essential. These fifteen members of the VEC elect the secretary and the chairperson, either of whom must be a woman. The Bihar State Vidyalaya Shiksha Samiti Act of 2000 defines the process for selection/expulsion of the VEC for a maximum term of three years. The studies done in the state of Bihar have shown that VECs did not have proper representation of women, scheduled castes and scheduled tribes and the minorities. The participation of district BEP officials and Block Education officer (BEO) was very poor in the process of formation of VECs. The members were mostly middle aged upper caste, educated, agriculturists. The awareness level about their role and functions, however, was below average. There was no coordination between VEC and *Mahila Samooh* in the village. There was a general lack of interest among members and there was lack of coordination between community, school and government functionaries (Lal: 1997). Inspite of the VECs under the Bihar Education Project, there are a number of issues which need to be addressed and looked into for strengthening the educational planning and management structure at the village level. To ensure that the right persons are elected to the VECs is a great difficulty since the influential and powerful people want to see themselves or their favourites as VEC members. The members did not even know the specific objectives of these bodies and no efforts were being made by anyone to ensure that good people come to these committees who work with interest and devotion. The *mukhiya* of the panchayat is not necessarily the right choice for president of a VEC. There was neither any formal mechanism for decision making nor there was any process for feed back to the VECs. One of the main difficulties which VECs face in performing their functions was that they didn't have any financial and administrative powers (Tyagi: 1999).

Experiences from Andhra Pradesh

In Andhra Pradesh, the schools committees have been constituted by the State Act no. 13 of 1998. The school committee consists of five members of whom four parents of the children enrolled in the school are the members. These parents are elected by all the parents of the children enrolled in the school. The head master or the senior teacher is the member convener of the school committee. Of the four parent members, at least two have to be women and one person has to be from scheduled caste community. The chairman is a parent. The term of office of the members of the school committee is two years. A parent member, however, ceases to be a member when he has no child enrolled in the school or when recalled by the parent-teacher association in the manner prescribed. The school committees in Andhra Pradesh are not the part of Gram Panchayats and are separate bodies.

The studies suggest that VECs in Vishakhapatnam District of Andhra Pradesh have been clearly involved in planning and implementation of educational intervention. More than 80 per cent heads of the household, even those who were not VEC members, attended the VEC meetings. There were cases where the VEC collected money from the community and paid salary to the teachers from the community funds (Sujatha and Rao: 2000).

Community participation in improving education is negligible in East Godavari district of Andhra Pradesh and members of the school education management committees have limited awareness of the Sarva Shiksha Abhiyan (SSA). An overwhelming majority (87.2%) of the school teachers were found to be aware of SSA, whereas in the case of PRI members, it was 61 per cent who were aware while among parents of the school-going children, 52 per cent were aware about Sarva Shiksha Abhiyan. The tribal community members were participating in some or the other way in the school-related activities. The community level structures i.e. the School Education Management Committees in this District of Andhra Pradesh played a key role in micro-planning, especially in the development of a village education plan and school improvement plans (Rao, Vasanta Srinivasa: 2009).

Experiences from Arunachal Pradesh

The Village Education Committees in the villages of Arunachal Pradesh has been constituted as per Govt. notification No.ED3/7/93, dated 21.6.93 with the objectives and guidelines of the revised Programme of Action 1992. The village education committee in this state consists of representatives from parents, panchayat, teachers, adult education instructors, cooperatives, women, local development functionaries. The total number of members does not exceed 15 in each village education committee. The village education committees in Arunachal Pradesh have been taking initiatives in education planning and development processes. The VECs are working for universal enrolment and retention of children in the schools. Overall, the working of VECs in Arunachal Pradesh has been satisfactory so far. The VECs in the state have organized various drives for increasing enrollment and retention of school children and the result had been impressive.

Experiences from Assam

Bhattacharya (2001) in the study on functioning of village education committees in selected VECs in Ghunucha cluster of Morigaon district of Assam found that all the sample VECs were constituted within the Government guidelines. All the VECs under study were formed in public meetings arranged by CRC co-coordinators or the Head teachers of primary schools of the villages. The composition of VECs was uniform and complied with the Government rules. The minimum qualification of president of VEC was fixed at matriculation and as a result, more than two-fifth (40%) VEC Presidents were replaced by qualified persons in the year 2000. Interestingly more than two-third of the total representatives of VECs were from Mothers' Committees. The mothers' committees appeared to be very active in the entire sampled VECs and more than half (50%) mothers' committees were fully involved in school as well as village development work. Nearly 70 per cent VECs were found to be active whereas in case of 30 per cent VECs, the working was not satisfied. However the VEC members along with the teachers prepared the action plan in most of the VECs in Assam in the year 2001.

Experiences from Kerala

Mathew (2001) found that the vicious circle of poverty compelled the poor parents not to participate in a satisfactory way in the school activities in Kerala. The role of Panchayat Raj Institutions with regard to monitoring has been significantly apprehended by the teaching community. The role of PRIs, in initiating quality improvement drives and cultural networking in the village, has remained far from satisfactory and there was a significant vacuum with regard to an integrated institutional mechanism at the panchayat level, which takes care of both the infrastructural as well as qualitative needs of the school. The different committees functioned as rather independent entities, with little or no give and take. On the other hand, there were no clear policies on primary education in the state, which swing the panchayats into action. The teaching community in Kerala obviously needs proper monitoring even as a few teachers had demonstrated excellent examples of meritorious work in this state.

Experiences from Odisha

Nayak (2002) found that a great majority of the members of VEC in Cuttack district don't attend the meetings of VEC regularly. There was no orientation among the members about the role and responsibilities of these committees. A great majority of these members did not approach the parents and convince them to send their children to school. Dash and Panda (2009) highlighted that most of the Village Education Committees in Nabarangpur district of Odisha worked excellently well for all round development of primary schools. All the VECs took care and management work of primary schools satisfactorily. VECs organized different awareness programmes satisfactorily for attitudinal change of villagers. Facilitation role of all VECs were very impressive. VECs undertook different steps to improve the financial status of primary schools. Proper care and management of primary schools, taking steps to increase enrolment and to reduce drop-out rate, organizing different cultural activities in schools, working for development of school environment and helping the teacher to prepare TLM were significant works of VEC, which significantly affected the environment of the local primary schools. Facilitation role, attitudinal role, school improvement role, economic activities and miscellaneous works have been performed by VECs effectively for all round development of the respective school. The study concluded that the role of VECs is very essential and important for the improvement of primary education. According to Nayak, P.M. (2009) people's direct participation in the management of primary education is very significant for materializing long cherished goal of universalisation of primary education. Specific efforts in various forms can be launched to revitalize the school-community relationships that can be gainfully channelized for quantitative as well as qualitative improvement of primary education in the country.

Experiences from Karnataka

In the state of Karnataka, the VECs are called as School Development and Management Committee (SDMC). SDMCs are a part of Gram Panchayat and chairman or a member elected from the village to gram panchayat is the chairman of the SDMC. Studies have shown that the involvement of community in academic activities for improvement of quality of primary education was not satisfactory in this state (Palakshiah: 1999). Government of Karnataka (2004) in collaboration with Azim Premji Foundation found out that 2 per cent of the schools in Karnataka didn't even have a School Development and Management Committee. The monitoring mechanism seemed to be ineffective. There was low representation of girls as student representatives in SDMCs. Students from SC/ST communities also need representation since they are still an underprivileged section. Vaijayanti (2005) recommends that SDMCs should be continued and their autonomy protected by insulating them against political interference -both in their formation and day-to-day functioning. There is ambiguity and confusion in the prevailing Government circular on the formation of SDMCs. Modifications suggested while retaining the content and spirit of the first executive order. There is a need involve SDMC members with reasonable qualifications (SSLC and above) in curriculum construction, teacher training and other academic issues at the school level.

Experiences from West Bengal

Village Education Committees in West Bengal have made contribution towards making sitting arrangements of students and improving the condition of school buildings and attendance of students at school. However, their frequency of visiting the school for the purpose of such supervision varied significantly. An analysis of the process of VEC formation makes it clear that there is no scope for the poorly educated people to be part of VEC. However unethical it may sound, probably it would not be desirable also to nominate such people as the decision-makers for issues related with education. However, they should be given the scope to voice their opinions, i.e., they should be empowered in case they are from socio-economically disadvantaged groups. The unstable economic capacity of people is often behind their poor participation in public works and dropout of their children from school. Therefore, one step towards empowering socio-economically disadvantaged population would be betterment of their economic strength. In this regard, gram panchayat may play a vital role through employment generation schemes as well as through poverty alleviation programmes. Significant amount of resources have already been spent in this regard. However, the majority of the efforts have been wasted due to improper vision and unplanned implementation. There is need to have frequent meetings between VEC functionaries, school teachers and the parents/guardians. A similar forum for discussing broader developmental issues is the meeting of gram sangsad (Wankhede and Sengupta: 2005). Sinha, Sujit (2007) while sharing the experiments of the NGO – Swanirvar in 24 Parganas district reiterated that encouraging parents to come to school during school hours and watch what their children were doing, proved very useful. The participation of the people in school activities was wonderful and in order to ensure even a better community participation in school governance, there is a need to reorient the bureaucrats, the state decision makers in matters of syllabus and text books, members of the inspectorate, the teachers' training institutes, and the existing teachers.

Experiences from Maharashtra

In Maharashtra, a Village Education Committee is constituted by the members elected by the Gram Sabha. Representation has been given to the Gram Panchayat on the Village Education Committee. Narayana and Chandrakant (2000) underlined that the co-ordination between the VEC and the higher authority like Block Level Education Authority or District level Education Authority in Satra district of Maharashtra was very less. The conduct of the meetings also needed improvement. In this district, it was observed that no proper notice was to be given by the Secretary of VEC to the members about the schedule of the meeting. There was inadequate representation of female and people belonging to reserved categories. The educational authorities had done little with regard to proper monitoring and mentoring the VEC meetings. No or very little attention was being paid towards conducting any training programmes for the VEC members.

Government of Maharashtra (2009) in its *Annual Work Plan and Budget Document* 2009-10 for Mid-day Meal (MDM) in Schools have fully authorized the Village Education Committees (VECs) to implement the scheme at school level. Funds are provided to the VECs and they have been given full powers to expand the scope of their working so as to improve the school education in the State. They have been empowered to inspect schools, maintenance and repair of building, creation of infrastructure at the school and community levels, monitoring the academic performance and attendance of children, supervising and monitoring the distribution of textbooks, ensuring drinking water and toilets, ensuring cleanliness and sanitation, ensuring proper utilization of grants and participation in all micro-planning processes. The Government in the *Annual Work Plan and Budget Document* 2009-10, has decided that the mid day meal scheme is to be implemented by the VECs at the village level, by the Ward Education Committees (WECs) at the municipal corporation or the urban level and the School Management Committees (SMCs) have to be responsible in the Private-Aided Schools for implementation of Mid Day Meal scheme. The VECs, WECs and the SMCs have been authorized to appoint Self Help Groups, *Mahila Mandals*, needy women or NGOs for full involvement of the community at various levels. Since the Mid Day Meals scheme has been totally decentralized, the community participation has increased tremendously in the state and this model has worked very well so far. Mother's involvement in supervision of cooked meals has helped children to participate in the school activities more actively.

Experiences from Nagaland

Village Education Committees have been constituted in respect of every village in the State of Nagaland. Village Education Committees have been given the responsibility of management of the schools located in the villages which include giving clearance for the release of monthly salary in respect of teachers, so as to regulate their attendance. Many primary school buildings have been constructed by way of community participation through the Village Development Boards. Decentralisation of education has been put to good use in villages where the community has consciously involved in the affairs of the school. This however is not the case all over the State. In many villages, changes have also taken place through the concern and effort of individuals. Trained and motivated teachers play a very big role in the process of decentralisation to sensitize village elders and parents so that they are not dependant wholly on the Government. Tongpangshilu (1990) is of the view that VECs in the State are doing good work to improve the standard of education in their respective villages through involvement of the people as far as possible. VEC made commendable efforts to involve the village people in most of the community based programmes apart from making them conscious of their children's welfare and responsibilities towards social change and upliftment.

Experiences from Haryana

The Village Education Committee normally comprises of 12 members (six males and six females). The Haryana Government in its guidelines for setting up village education committees suggested that three members to VEC are to be nominated by the Gram Panchayat, of which, atleast one has to be from scheduled castes community and one has to be a woman member. The Head of the primary school in the village will act as member secretary of the committee. One lady teacher is to be nominated by the headmaster/headmistress apart from one representative of Mahila Mandal is to be recommended by the Mandal. One Multi-purpose health worker (female) is also to be a member of the VEC. Besides these, an anganwadi worker (Bal Sevika), two parents of children to be nominated by Parent Teacher Association (PTA)/Mother Teacher Association (MTA, one person from voluntary organization or a social worker nominated by Block Education Officer and Village Secretary/Gram Sevika also the members of the VEC in the state of Haryana.

In order to operationalize participatory decentralized model of development with community initiative, the people are to be made primary agent of their own development through education and organization. Development at grassroots level cannot be achieved without the participation of the community. The Village Education Committees (VECs) play a vital role in the improvement of enrolment of children. These committees ensure greater retention and reduce the drop-out rates. The VECs have emerged as effective instruments for people's involvement in the school management in the State (Menon: 1996).

The participation of women is limited in terms of the actual role in the functioning of VEC. The women still observed *purdah* and many of them do not even look up to male members and speak. This reticence and non-participation of women effect the functioning of the VECs as many of the local issues remain unaddressed. In some cases, however, the woman *pradhan*, who is usually an elderly woman, was more vocal. There is a visible change in the attitudes towards girls' education (Menon: 1999). As per the study by Yadav (2006) only those member should be nominated who are at least matriculate and there must be a fixed tenure for each member. It should be made mandatory for all members to attend the meetings. Community leaders should extend full cooperation to VECs for better functioning of the schools. From the above experiences, it can be said that there have mixed bag of experiences. Just as there are failures, there are success stories too. On the whole, community in the form of Panchayats, Parent-Teacher Associations and Village Education Development Committees (VEDC) is very important for managing the school affairs. Inspite of the failures, the involvement of community through Village Education Committees has given a good start in operationalizing the participatory decentralized model of development in all kinds of activities of the school like enrolment, teaching learning processes, organizing different cultural activities and maintaining a clean school environment. In general, community participation as a process has created a space of its own so far as school governance at the grassroots is concerned.

Summing Up

The participatory management of schools involving communities has been recognized as a crucial aspect in almost all Indian States. The on-going Sarva Shiksha Abhiyan (SSA) strives to achieve community participation through Village Educational Committees (VECs) with specific mandate that include enhancing enrolment and retention, micro planning and school management, fiscal responsibility and accountability for bringing improvement in the quality of education in elementary schools. The Programme is being implemented all across the Country. Community participation in education through Village Educational Committees has been given utmost importance in most policy documents of the state governments. VECs have given various powers, functions and funds for improving the school governance apart from creating adequate infrastructural facilities in the school. It is clear from the evidences captured in the foregoing discussion that the experience on performance of VECs in term of meeting their intended goals have been mixed.

5

The Manifesto of Participatory Management of Schools in Punjab

Being fully aware of the social commitments, the Government of Punjab is leaving no stone unturned to ensure that all communities get access to and the advantage of educational facilities. The Government has introduced programmes to provide free and compulsory education to all children in the age group of 6-14 years as mandated by the Government of India. Giving unqualified priority to school education, the State Government has introduced various innovative approaches like mobilizing community support and introducing decentralized planning to help achieve the goal of universalisation of elementary education. Incentives such as stipends and scholarships, free books and uniforms and mid-day meals etc have been initiated in all government schools in order to improve the attendance and to boost overall literacy. The Sarva Shiksha Abhiyan (SSA) which hinges around decentralized planning and community participation is being religiously implemented by the Government of Punjab since 2002. SSA has empowered the local community by their involvement in all aspects of plan formulation. Community based planning process is being carried out by delegating powers to Panchayati Raj Institutions and constituting the Village Education Development Committees (VEDCs). The equity issues related to girls and children from socially disadvantaged groups and with special needs are being properly attended under the Programme. The Programme has helped bridge the social gaps and to a great extent ensured that no child aged 6-14 years remains out-of-school in the State. Since the implementation of the Programme, there has been a visible impact on the school infrastructure as well as quality of school education (GoI: 2000). Considerable progress has been on access related in terms of getting out of school children in to the school and ensuring that they stay there. The quality dimensions of school education are also being addressed by ensuring that the teachers are present and quality teaching learning takes place. Broad strategies under the SSA are institutional reforms in order to improve the efficiency of delivery systems and to reach out to the educationally deprived children across all communities (GoI: 2000). The present chapter gives an elaborate account of the general norms/rules of working of VEDCs as framed by the Sarva Shiksha Abhiyan Authority, Govt. of Punjab from time to time. These rules are primarily compiled from documents, circulars, reports and orders etc. of the state Government.

Village Education Development Committees* in Punjab: Guiding the Course of Community Participation

Village Education Committees (VECs) known as Village Education Development Committees (VEDCs) or in Punjabi addressed as Pendu Sikhiya Vikas Committees (Pasvak) were formally announced in October 2002 by the then Education Minister of Punjab in the Congress Government Mr. Kushal Behal. After the announcement, the VEDCs actually started functioning only after the panchayat elections held in June 2003. The VEDCs in the State are expected to be helpful in improving the standard of school education in the village through community involvement. Formation of these bodies has legitimately ensured people' participation in the school related activities at the village level by involving the teachers, parents, women representatives and social activists. The VEDCs act local management committees for each school which actively participate in the development activities of a school and implement them. VEDCs are viewed as a medium to accelerate the pace of development of primary education in the State. The VEDCs provide representation to both the elected local bodies like PRIs and the common people. A VEDC consists of eight members. Two members are from the village panchayat, two members are from the PTA, one member each has to be an ex-

* In compliance to RTE Act 2009, the VEDCs in Punjab have been renamed as School Management Committees (SMCs) with effect from April 01, 2012.

military personnel, a philanthropist/NRI and a retired teacher of the Government of Punjab. The Head teacher of the concerned school is the Secretary of the VEDC. The composition of VEDC has been, however, amended in 2010. The new guidelines regarding composition of VEDCs along with the details related to the process of formation, nomination and the functions of these bodies would be discussed in details in subsequent Chapter.

Preamble of VEDC

1. Resources by the State and the community but management by VEDC.
2. Teachers to be paid by the Government but they would show path of guidance to our children.
3. Barrier-free education policy formulation by each household.
4. Each household means the house of the poorest of the poor, the house of the deprived, the house of the oppressed and the house of each one of us.
5. The VEDC is of all and for all.

Goals of VEDC

1. To intimate institutional reforms in the quality of school education in the State.
2. Effective decentralization upto school level.
3. Right of the community in school management through peoples' initiatives.
4. Community based plan formulation and implementation for the development of school education.
5. Flexible programme formulation for the school development as per the local needs.
6. To encourage participation of the people, local, state and central governments for capital investment towards spread of education.
7. To development appropriate methods of spending with the involvement of local people.
8. To have social audit of the expenditures through people-based evaluation and to bring transparency in school expenditures.
9. To motivate teachers through better management systems and effective ways of learning.

10. To develop inclusive, effective and relevant methods for improving the academic standards through local people.
11. To give priority to special efforts for the education of children.
12. To help design context-specific programmes for Scheduled Castes, Scheduled Tribes children and the children from the sections living below poverty line.
13. To provide special education facilities to children with special needs.
14. To establish linkages with *Anganwadi* programmes.
15. To make education relevant to life through real-life experiences.
16. To ensure quality of all programmes so that a child-friendly joyful education can be encouraged that emphasize on methods of learning by doing, hearing and seeing.

General Rules of Working: According to the guidelines of 2010, the Chairman of VEDC is to be elected by majority from amongst the VEDC members excluding the ex-officio members. For nominating the PRI members, the village Panchayat passes a resolution to this effect and sends it to the head teacher. The tenure of PRI members as the members of VEDC is co-terminus with the tenure of the Panchayat. With the formation of new Panchayat, new nominations are required to be done. Likewise the nominations of the PTA members are done by the school PTA by passing a resolution. Only those PTA members are nominated to VEDC whose children study in that particular school. PTA members remain the members of the VEDC till such time they are members the PTA. The nomination of ex-serviceman, philanthropist, retired teacher and the senior-most teacher is done by the head master. For ex-serviceman, the highest rank and length of service is given preference. As philanthropist such person from amongst the villagers is nominated who donations to the school are highest. The senior-most teacher from among the school-staff excluding the head master is also the member of the VEDC. The senior-most teacher is authorized to act as the secretary of VEDC in the absence the head teacher. The formation of VEDC is finally sent to the DEO (Elementary Education) for approval by the head teacher. The DEO (Elementary Education) approves the formation and sends it back to the head teacher. The tenure of VEDC is of three years from the date of approval by the DEO (Elementary Education).

The VEDC can change any unfit member by passing a resolution, but such change can be made only with the prior approval of the DEO (Elementary Education). In case, any member of the committee remains absent in three consecutive meetings, his membership is cancelled and a new member is nominated in his place. In any case, the position of any VEDC member cannot remain vacant for more than three months. The monthly meeting of VEDC is compulsory. If need arises more than one meeting can also be held. This meeting is held in the school as per pre-decided date and time. The notice of the meeting is issued by the member secretary. The quorum of the VEDC meeting is essentially 1/3 of the total members. The VEDC meeting or any other work of the Committee cannot remain interrupted due to the absence of a member. The VEDC is fully authorized to take any appropriate decision in the interest of the school. The VEDC can pass resolution for all the works to be undertaken in future. Every resolution shall have to have the signatures of each participating member. It is the responsibility of the member secretary to record the minutes of the meetings and the passed resolutions in the school register. The VEDC has to open a separate account for the grants received from SSA. This account is jointly operated by the member secretary and the chairman. The VEDC chairman or any other member of the VEDC shall not, in any case, ask to bring any school record outside the school premises. The VEDC meeting is to be held within the school only. For signing any document or a cheque, the VEDC chairman has to himself come to the school. If such a thing is not done or observed, the member secretary has to report the matter to the district head quarter. On the basis of this report, the DEO can issue a show cause notice to the concerned chairman or member and in case of an unjustified explanation, he/she can be removed from the position. It is the sole responsibility of the member secretary to maintain the accounts and get all SSA work and activities completed as per the guidelines.

System of Working of VEDC: The VEDC has to hold at least one meeting between 2nd and 7th day every month. The record of the resolutions passed in these meetings has to be essentially maintained. The VEDC is authorized to undertake works requiring an estimated expenditure up to Rs. 15, 00,000. The Government would provide the designs and the estimates of construction work to the VEDC and give required suggestions during the process of construction. Besides this, the Government would also help the VEDC in maintaining records of all the civil/construction works done by it in the village. The VEDC need not float tenders of the works falling within its authorized limits. The VEDC is also authorized to spend the grant/funds given to it by the Government from time to time. The Department of Education, from time to time, gives directions to the VEDC with regard to the Designs, the Drawings, the Estimates and the constructions of different types of civil works in the school. The VEDC make all arrangements for constructions/civil works as per the technical recommendations in relation to the scope, design and the specifications.

For effective implementation and sustainability of different on-going projects, the VEDC on its own, by passing resolution, may form as many sub-committees of its members as required. The VEDC can include members with technical and other leadership skills from the village for a fixed tenure and for a particular work. At least half of such members have to be women. All the decisions of such sub-committees are to be passed in the VEDC meetings. Each resolution of the VEDC has to be signed by atleast five members out of which two have to be female members of the VEDC.

Local Construction Committees: The VEDC, by passing a resolution in the meeting in each case, can constitute as many Local Construction Committees (LCCs) for monitoring and supervision of each ongoing civil work. The decisions taken by the LCC have to be essentially presented and passed in the monthly meetings of the VEDC. The members of the LCC have to be the VEDC Chairman, Head teacher of school who is also the member secretary of VEDC, the ex-servicemen or the retired teacher of Punjab Government, one female PTA member, another PTA member (male/female) and two members from the village with technical skills. The Local Construction Committee essentially has to have at least two women members.

Utilization of Grants/Funds by the VEDC

As per the guidelines of the Department of Education, Government of Punjab, all the grants/funds received for school development are to be deposited in the account of the VEDC which is jointly operated by the VEDC Chairman and the member secretary. For operating the joint account, there is no need to seek approval from the DEO. All the payments exceeding Rs. 500/- are to be made by cheque signed both by the VEDC Chairman and the Head teacher of the school. No work is to be undertaken by the VEDC without passing a resolution in the VEDC meeting. The VEDC participate in the planning of developmental activities for the school and monitor every aspect related to their effective implementation. The VEDC ensures proper utilization and upkeep of the projects material. Before starting a development project, the VEDC has to enter into a Memorandum of Understanding (MoU). The MoU has to be signed by the DEO (Primary) on behalf of the State Government and the Chairman of the VEDC on behalf of the VEDC. The funds approved by the Government for the works to be undertaken by the VEDC are to be deposited in the joint account of the VEDC Chairman and the Head teacher. VEDC has to ensure that the village people make contribution towards school activities in cash or by donating land so that maximum participation of the people can be facilitated in the school development. The grants have to be utilized only as per the financial procedures. The outstanding amount, after utilization of the grant for specific purpose, can be used for other activities of the school development by passing a resolution in the VEDC meeting. The involvement of a contractor is strictly prohibited in the works undertaken by the VEDC.

Rules for Utilization of Grants/Funds for Construction/Civil Works: Before initiating any work and for the estimated expenditures on such work, the VEDC has to pass a resolution to this effect. The Head teacher of the school has to create detailed record of the expenditures on each work involved. It is the responsibility of the Head teacher to keep the relevant records of expenses with him and the same shall remain readily available for inspection by the Block Primary Education Officer/DEO (Elementary Education). At the time of withdrawal of money from the joint account, the VEDC Chairman and the Head teacher have to prepare a statement of the expenses to be incurred on a specific work. Advance money cannot be withdrawn without any specific need. All work related payments are made under the signatures of the VEDC Chairman and the Head teacher. Both of them individually, as well as jointly, are responsible for any kind of discrepancy with regard to the expenses on any work or loss or any other such errors. Every voucher/receipt relating to any expenditure amount has to have the number and the date of the resolution passed in this regard. The Chairman VEDC and the Head Teacher are responsible for keeping the actual payee receipt (APR)/voucher in safe custody along with the records of the VEDC. Both of them are responsible for safe custody of the Cash Book and Stock Register etc. Before starting any construction work, a photograph is to be clicked showing the space and the surroundings. Photographs have also to be clicked before the slab and after completion of the construction work which are to be readily available in the records for checking. The committee constituted by the Department of Education for fixing and examining the rates of wages and inspecting the necessary construction material has to hold its meeting from time to time. The guidelines are issued from time to time for keeping proper accounts of the purchases and the expenditure incurred by the VEDC and the VEDC has to adhere to these guidelines accordingly.

Monitoring the Progress of Works: The monitoring of all civil/construction or other works undertaken by the VEDC are to be done on the basis of the monthly progress reports. The Block, District and State level officials from time to time, inspect the ongoing works of the VEDC.

Progress Reports of VEDC

a) *School Level*: The Head teacher prepares a progress report of the ongoing works of the VEDC on the prescribed performa. The progress report is presented in the monthly meetings. After the approval by the VEDC, the progress report is sent to the Cluster Resource Centre (CRC) under the signatures of the VEDC Chairman and the Head teacher.
b) *CRC Level*: CRC coordinator compile all the progress reports of various VEDCs on prescribed performa and sends them, under his signatures, to the block officer within next two days. CRC coordinator himself inspect the ongoing works atleast once in a month and record his observations in the Inspection Book.
c) *BPEO Level*: The BPEO, on receiving the reports from CRC

coordinators, compile the reports on the prescribed performa and sends them, under signature, to the DEO within next two days. The BPEO himself inspect the ongoing works of the VEDC at least once in three months and records his observations in the Inspection Book.

d) *District level*: The District Education Officer compiles all the reports received from the Block Level on prescribed performa and sends them, under signatures, to the main office within next two days. He inspects the ongoing works himself or through his nominee at least once in six months and record the suggestions in the Inspection Book of the school.
e) *State Level*: The SPD-SSA has to compile all the reports and inspect them. He himself or through his nominee inspect the ongoing works of the VEDCs of at least 10 per cent of the schools.

Annual Reports of VEDC

1. At the end of the year, the VEDC has to prepare an Annual Report listing all the grants received from different sources along with the statement of utilization or underutilization of each grant. The Annual Report has to include the details of the works planned for the next year along with the estimated expenditures likely to incur on each of these works.
2. The annual report has to be signed both by the Head teacher and the VEDC Chairman. A copy of this report is sent to the CRC by the VEDC.
3. Each CRC has to compile the annual reports received from the VEDCs and send the consolidated annual reports of each cluster to the BEO (Primary).
4. The BEO (primary) has to consolidate the annual reports of the CRCs and send the consolidated report, under his signatures, to the DEO (Primary.
5. The DEO (Primary) receive the reports from the BEOs (Primary) and consolidate them. Thereafter, the DEO (Primary) has to inspect the ongoing works accordingly. Then the DEO (Primary) with his comments has to send the reports to the SPD who, thereafter, has to send the annual progress reports and the quarterly progress reports

of the ongoing works to the State and the Central Governments.

System of Audit: The works of VEDC has to be socially as well as legally audited. For social audit, the VEDC has to put up a display board in the school or at any other common place under the name of the VEDC Chairman which shows the details of the grants, name of works, estimated costs, starting date of work, material purchased and the completion date. The display board is to be updated on daily basis with the details of day to day activities. The VEDC has to keep an inspection book which should remain available during the visits of the concerned officials of the Department. The suggestions of the department officials as recorded in the inspection book shall have to be essentially complied with by the VEDC Chairman and the Head teacher of the school. The VEDC has to essentially hold a meeting between 2nd to 7th of every month to share information with other members regarding the expenditures and the status of ongoing works. The VEDC has to convene at least two meetings of Gram Sabha in a year in which the statement of expenditure incurred and details of the grants received would be presented. Suggestions will have to be sought from the village people for school development and for improving the standards of education. Appropriate decision has to be taken on these suggestions is the next VEDC meeting.

Legal Audit of the work done by the VEDC: The accounts of the VEDC are to be audited by a Chartered Accountant authorized by the Department of Audit. Apart from that, the Controller Auditor General would audit VEDC accounts from time to time as per the rules of the State as well as the Central government. The Department of Education, Government of Punjab would continue to issue instructions and guidelines to the VEDCs which would essentially be complied by the VEDCs in letter and spirit.

Guidelines for Civil Works: For universalisation of elementary education, SSA Punjab provides financial grants for different aspects of school education. One among many such aspects are the civil works for which the grants are provided for construction of building in schools without building, for additional classrooms as needed for the schools having less number of classrooms, for verandah for the schools without verandah, for water tank for the safe drinking water for children and for construction of sanitary block for hygienic toilets for the boys and the girls. All such grants are utilized only under the heads/items for which they are released. All the funds released under the civil work schemes are to be deposited in the account jointly operated the VEDC chairman and the Head teacher. The approval of the DEO is not required for operating this joint account. The payments exceeding Rs. 500 are to be done by a cheque only. Every bill/receipt of payments has to be essentially signed by both of the VEDC Chairman and the Head teacher. Withdrawal of cash from this account and keeping the cash as an advance for any estimated expenditure is not allowed in any case. The Head teacher has to enter the grants received for civil works in the income side of the Cash Book and under the same Head as it is received. The amount spent from this head would be entered in the expense side of the Cash Book. The details of the income and the expenditure would be maintained systematically and properly. The bills of expenses and the receipts of payments would be enclosed date-wise in an office file. To ensure the authenticity of these receipts, each bill and receipt would have to be signed by the VEDC Chairman, Head teacher and a VEDC member.

The resolution number along with the date, under which the VEDC has sanctioned the particular amount of expenditure, is to be mentioned on each bill/receipt. The details of each receipt, bill and cheque has to be entered on the expenditure side of the Cash Book. The resolution number and the date shall also have to be entered in the Cash Book. The Head teacher has to prepare the Cash Book of each year which is inspected by the appropriate officials from time to time. The inspecting officer tallies the bills of receipts with the Cash Book and signs on each bill and receipt with date. In case, the officer finds any gap in the Cash Book, he has to record his remarks in the Cash Book under his signatures and date. On the closing date of every month, the VEDC Chairman, Head teacher and one VEDC member have to sign on the Cash Book after calculating the total income, the total expenditure and the net difference.

Approval for Utilization of Funds: The VEDC has to convene a meeting which discusses the details of the works to be undertaken. The proceedings/minutes of the meeting are to be recorded in the Register and the decisions taken on each item are to be recorded separately. Resolution number and date are to be recorded for every decision according to which the civil works would be undertaken and respective expenditure would be done.

Estimated Expenditure as per the Approved List of Civil Works: After the VEDC approval for utilization of funds, the secretary/ Head teacher would prepare an estimate of expenditure likely to be incurred on the approved civil work planned to be started. The details of the estimated expenditure would be discussed in the VEDC meeting and necessary action would be taken. After passing the resolution of approval of the estimated expenditure, the VEDC would constitute a Local Constitution Committee for starting and monitoring the work as listed. The Local Constitution Committee would take all decisions on all pre-decided construction works and expenditures under the authority of VEDC, as per the rules. However, the Committee shall seek approval from the VEDC before implementing its decisions.

The Power and Authority of the VEDC for Civil Works

1. The VEDC is authorized to undertake works upto Rs. 15,00,000 along with the Government grants/funds. The VEDC need to invite tenders for works which are within its authority. The VEDC is fully authorised to spend all the grants/funds received by it.
2. The involvement of a contractor in the civil work to be initiated by the VEDC is strictly prohibited. The VEDC shall not give any work on contract.
3. The VEDC is fully authorized to purchase any material relating to the construction work.
4. VEDC is authorized to hire masons and labourer for the construction work. For this purpose, the VEDC is not required to seek approval from any other institution.

Responsibilities of VEDC for Civil Works

1. VEDC can purchase the best material with least cost for all construction works.
2. VEDC has to ensure that the construction works are done in appropriate concrete mixture/mortar.
3. For monitoring and supervision of the construction work, the VEDC has to constitute a Local Construction Committee.
4. VEDC has to invite at least three quotations and purchase

good quality material from good vendors/shops and make all possible efforts to have the cheap and the best material.

5. VEDC has to make efforts so as to involve cheap but skilled masons and labourers and those who are able to understand the technical details and designs and are able to complete the work as per technical specifications.
6. VEDC has to ensure that the necessary guidelines as issued by the Education Department from time to time with regards to designs, drawings, estimates and construction are complied with. The VEDC has to make necessary arrangements to carry out the constructions work as per the technical specifications including the estimates and designs.
7. In case, the VEDC feels the need to carry out some improvement or modifications with regards to the estimates, designs and drawings etc. then the VEDC can do so after calling a meeting and passing a resolution to that effect.
8. VEDC has to ensure that the grants are utilized as per the specific terms and conditions.
9. After completion of the work for which the grant was received, if some amount remains unspent, in that case, the unspent amount can be used for any other developmental work after passing a resolution to that effect.
10. VEDC has to ensure that before initiating any construction work, a photograph must be clicked showing the place and its surrounding areas. Photographs will also be taken before the slab and after the completion of construction which will always have to be readily available in the records for inspection.

Purchase of Material: The Government guidelines state that once the resolution regarding the estimated cost/expenditure is passed, the VEDC has to prepare a list of the items/materials required for construction. Thereafter, the VEDC would prepare a list of sources/ firms/vendors from where different material/items of good quality can be procured or such firms/vendors which have a good reputation in the market with regard to the cost and quality of the construction material. At least three quotations are to be invited from different sources/firms/vendors for procuring the required construction material. At the time of taking the quotation, the firms, vendors or the suppliers of the construction material are to be informed that the payments would be made within two days of receiving the appropriate material. The firms/vendors are to be informed about the quality and the specification of the constructions material.

After having received all the quotations relating to all the required material, the Local Construction Committee has to prepare the details of comparative rates of the three quotations received for each material-item in a register which has to be produced before the VEDC chairman and the VEDC secretary for approval. After recording the quantity, quality and the specifications, a written order of supply would be sent to the firm which has quoted the lowest rates as per the quality and the specifications.

After receiving the supply of the material, the Local Construction Committee (LCC) has to tally all the items as per the supply order and certify on the bill that the material supplied is according to the quantity, quality and the specifications. All the supplied material is to be stored at an appropriate place. It is responsibility of the Head teacher to prepare the Stock Register and keep it in the safe custody. Apart from different construction items purchased, the entries of all other items as purchased are also to be made in this stock register. Separate page has to be maintained for separate items. Another Stock Register named as Stock Register (material at site) is also be prepared at the construction site. The main stock register remains with the Head teacher and it is prepared and taken care of by the head teacher only. Whereas, the Stock Register (material at site) is prepared and taken care of by any of the members of the Local Construction Committee. This register is kept at the construction site and the details of the material issued by the Head teacher for a particular work are entered into this register. The register provides the details of the materials used on daily-basis and also of the materials lying at the construction site.

Transparency in Civil Work

1. VEDC has to put up a display board in the school or at any other common place showing the details of grants received, name of work head, estimated cost of work, starting date, costs of material purchased, finish date etc.

under the name of the VEDC Chairman. It has to be updated on daily-basis.

2. VEDC shall have to prepare an Inspection Book which has to remain available at the time of visits of the Departmental officials. It is responsibility of the Head teacher and the VEDC Chairman to ensure that the suggestions/orders as recorded by the Departmental officials in the Inspection Book are complied with.
3. VEDC has to convene a monthly meeting between 2nd and 7th of every month to share the information with the VEDC members regarding the progress of the work and the money spent on construction.
4. VEDC has to convene at least two meetings of the Gram Sabha in a year in which the details of the grants and the expenditures are to be presented. VEDC has to prepare and present utilization certificates of each grant.
5. The accounts of VEDC are to be audited by the Education Department from a certified Chartered Accountant. Apart from that, the C.A.G. shall also audit the accounts as per the guidelines of the Government of Punjab and the Central Government.

Inspection of the Progress of Civil Work: Inspection of the progress of the civil work undertaken by the VEDC is to be continuously done at the site. Inspection has also to be done on the basis of the monthly progress report. The block, district and state level officials shall, from time to time, make visits to monitor the progress of the civil works. The monthly progress reports are to be prepared at different levels and be sent to the higher officials for inspection of the progress of the ongoing works.

1. At school level, the Head teacher has to prepare a progress report in the prescribed Performa. This report is to be presented in the monthly meeting of the VEDC. After the approval of the VEDC, the Head teacher and VEDC chairman sign and send this report to the CRC.
2. The CRC coordinator has to compile all the reports received from various schools on the prescribed Performa and send the consolidated report to the BEO (Elementary Education) within two days under his signatures. The CRC

coordinator would have to inspect the ongoing works himself atleast once in a month and record his comments in the school Inspection Book with his signatures and date.

3. The BEO (Elementary Education) has to compile all the reports received from the CRC coordinators on the prescribed Performa and send the consolidated report to the DEO (Elementary Education) with two days under his signatures. The BEO (Elementary Education) has to inspect the ongoing works himself at least once in three months and record his comments in the school Inspection Book under his signatures with date.
4. The DEO (Elementary Education) has to compile all the reports received from various blocks on the prescribed Performa and send the consolidated report to the main office with in two days under his signatures. He has to inspect the ongoing works himself or send his nominee at least once in six months and record his comments in the school Inspection Book with his signatures and date.
5. At the state level, the State Project Director -SSA has to compile all the reports and inspect the ongoing works of the VEDC in at least 10 per cent of the total schools in the state.

Sources of Income of VEDC: The VEDC, from time to time, receive grants from Central/State Governments, Local Governments etc. Apart from that, VEDC receive grants/finds/donations/help from the following sources:

1. Any grant from Government of Punjab/grant under any scheme
2. Any grant from Central Government/grant under any scheme e.g. Sarva Shiksha Abhiyan and JRY etc.
3. Any grant from the District Planning and Development Board.
4. Help received from Panchayat.
5. Any grant/help from Chief Minister or any other minister of Central/State Governments.
6. Help received from industrialists and businessmen.
7. Help received from individuals or institutions.
8. Help received from PTA
9. Any other source.

The accounts of the grants/funds from above sources are to be maintained by the VEDC in the Cash Book in a systematic and proper manner.

Grants Received by VEDC and Methods of Utilization: The records of the grants received from various sources are to be maintained by the VEDC chairman and the secretary. The accounts are to be maintained by the secretary but it is the responsibility of the VEDC chairman to ensure that the details of the grants received and the accounts of expenditures are maintained systematically and properly. Before actually spending any funds on the proposed works, the VEDC essentially has to pass a resolution regarding the estimated expenditures likely to be incurred on the developmental works proposed to be undertaken by the VEDC. The VEDC is not allowed to undertake any work, nor can it utilize any grant without passing a resolution.

It is the responsibility of the VEDC secretary to present the details of the grants/funds received, the expenditures done in the monthly as well as the annual meetings and get them passed accordingly. After getting it passed in the monthly meeting, it is the responsibility of the VEDC secretary to send the monthly report to the coordinator of the concerned CRC. In order to maintain the accounts of the VEDC, the funds have been as under.

i. *New Construction:* The VEDC has to utilize the grants/funds on the purchase of material essential for the construction of school building like bricks, cement, steel etc. and the cost of their transport and labour; on electric goods and wood and the cost of labour on them; on the cost of labour and the rent of the hired objects/material. VEDC can receive land in donation from Panchayat or other individual and shall not purchase the land, in any case. As far as possible, the building shall be constructed with the collaboration of the village people so that the possible contribution of the volunteers can be solicited and the expenditures on transport and labour can be avoided to the maximum extent. This will instill a sense of trust in the people that the constructed building belongs to them.

ii. *Repairs*: The VEDC has to carry out repairs of the old buildings of the school like the roof, walls, floors, doors, windows, ventilators, four-walls and main gate etc. Apart from that, the VEDC has to work for the upkeep and repair of the materials like the furniture, fittings and other infrastructural facilities available and used in the school.

iii. *Purchases*: The VEDC can make purchases relating to office and classroom furniture, blackboards, teaching and learning material, sports goods, furniture, almirahs, books, newspapers and magazines for the library.

iv. *Honorarium/Remuneration*: The VEDC can make payments of honorarium to the workers/volunteers/service providers employed for the EGS centres, Balwaris, for special drives for education of SC and ST children, for art-clubs, as education volunteers, for learning of soft skills to the children and other extra curricular activities etc.

v. *Miscellaneous Expenditures*: In order to achieve its objectives and for completion of its works, the VEDC can also spend grants/funds for different other expenditures like making payments of water and electricity bills, sanitation and beautification of surroundings, preparation of playground, planting trees and shrubs within and around the school, help the needy children, educational tours, cultural programmes, medicines to students during emergencies and first aids etc.

It is the responsibility of the VEDC to keep and maintain accounts of income and expenditures in a systematic and proper manner. Attention is again invited towards the fact that VEDC can not do any expenditure without passing a resolution to that effect. No work would be started with out passing a resolution, nor would any expenditure be done.

It is the responsibility of the Head teacher to prepare and maintain the Cash Book for incomes and expenditures of the VEDC. He has to paste and carefully keep all the vouchers and receipts of expenditures in an office file in a chronological order. Every bill/voucher/receipt shall be signed by the VEDC chairman, Head teacher and a member of the VEDC so that their safe upkeep can be assured. Every receipt has to bear the resolution number and the date by which the said expenditure has been approved.

It is the responsibility of the Head teacher to prepare the Cash Book for the financial year and get it verified by the appropriate official from time to time. Each verifying official has to sign on the

Cash Book with date as a proof that the verification has been done. Besides signing the Cash Book, the verifying official would also sign on each voucher with date. In case the verifying official finds a gap/error, he shall record his comments in the Cash Book.
Every month the VEDC would present the details of the income and expenditures in its progress report. The VEDC would record the details of the balance amount from a particular grant received during that period.

From the discussion, it is clear that the community participation in the form of Village Education Development Committee (VEDC), Panchayats, Parent-Teacher Association is very important for managing the school affairs. These bodies give a right to the parents to choose the kind of education that their children should get. The Government of India has empowered these bodies to inspect schools, monitor the academic performance of children, attendance and quality of education, supervise regular supply of quality and hygienic mid-day meals, supervise and monitor aspects relating to distribution of textbooks, maintenance and repair of building, creation of infrastructure at the school and community levels, ensuring drinking water and toilets, ensuring cleanliness and sanitation, ensuring the proper utilization of grants, participation in micro-planning process and organizing community mobilization activities for developing better coordination between various stakeholders. The school-community partnership in education in form of Village Education Committees has, to a great extent, increased the relevance and quality of education, improved ownerships and built institutional capacities in the Country.

6

The Vehicles of Community Participation: Structure, Functions and Functionaries

Sarva Shiksha Abhiyan has put great emphasis on community based planning by delegating powers to Panchayati Raj Institutions and constituting the Village Education Committees (VECs) at village level. Under SSA quality and equity issues have been mandated to be attended by these bodies. The Right to Education 2009 has also envisaged the constitution of School Management Committee for the day to day governance of the village schools. The quality dimensions of school education are expected to be addressed by ensuring that the community people actively participate in the teaching learning process.

In Punjab, Village Education Committees are named as Village Education Development Committees, in short, VEDCs. As has been pointed out earlier that after RTE Act 2009, they have been renamed as School Management Committees (SMCs) with effect from April 01, 2012. These committees have been formed to act as the vehicles of community participation since their launch in the year 2003. The present chapter presents an elaborate account of the process of formation, composition and functions of these committees. It also takes stock of the socio-economic profile and awareness level of the members of the VEDCs. The analysis of formation, composition and functions of these committees has been carried out primarily from the secondary sources largely consisting of the documents, reports, circulars and guidelines of the State as well as the Central Government. In order to know the socio-economic profile and the awareness of the VEDC members, primary data has been collected with the help of pre-designed structured Interview Schedules. All the members of Village

Education Development Committees (VEDC) and the teachers of the rural primary schools of the state of Punjab formed the population of the present study. The members of Village Education Development Committees include head teachers, members of the village panchayats, member of the respective parent–teacher associations, retired teachers, ex-servicemen, and philanthropists/ NRIs.

According to DISE (2008-2009) in the state of Punjab, there are 12279 government rural primary schools out of the total 19326 government schools (primary, upper primary, secondary and senior secondary). Since under Sarva Shiksha Abhiyan (SSA), it is mandatory for every government elementary school to have a village education development committee to ensure community participation for smooth functioning of the village school, the members of all the 12279 Village Education Development Committees (VEDCs) made for the rural government primary schools forms the population of this study. In order to collect valid and reliable data about the functioning of the VEDCs, the researcher employed multi-stage purposive-cum-stratified random sampling. After selecting the two lowest literacy districts, villages, village schools, VEDCs, members of the VEDCs and the school teachers formed different units taken into consideration for drawing the sample for this study. As such, a village has been the principle unit while the VEDC and the village school formed the second unit of sampling. The members of VEDCs and the teachers formed the final unit of sampling for the present study.

For selection of districts, the criterion followed was the level of literacy. Since the study is proposed to be carried out in the educationally backward districts, the researcher purposively selected two most educationally backward districts with the lowest the literacy rates (as per the Census 2001) from among all the districts of the state of Punjab. This way district Mansa and Muktsar were identified as the two districts for carrying out this study. As per the Census 2001, the literacy rate of Mansa is the lowest with 52.4 per cent while that of Muktsar is the second lowest with 58.2 per cent as against 69.7 per cent for the state of Punjab.

For the drawing the sample of villages, the list of villages of both the districts (Mansa and Muktsar) were accessed from the Census 2001 data. In Mansa, there are 237 villages while in Muktsar there are 233 villages. As per the DISE data 2007-2008, there were

466 schools in District Mansa of which 291 were primary, 82 upper primary and the rest 93 schools were upper primary with secondary/senior secondary schools. Of these schools, 341 were managed by the Department of Education, Govt of Punjab while 124 were being managed by the Panchayats and one by local body. Across Muktsar District there were 521 schools consisting 321 primary schools, 74 upper primary schools and 126 upper primary with secondary/senior secondary schools. In this district 408 schools were managed by Department of Education, Govt of Punjab while 111 were being managed by the Panchayats and 02 were managed by local body.

For the sample, a total of 52 villages as per required indices, have been selected from both the districts (26 villages from District Mansa and 26 villages from District Muktsar). The selection of a village eventually led to the selection of a school and the respective Village Education Development Committee (VEDC). Ultimately 52 rural primary schools and 52 VEDCs were studied for the present investigation.

For drawing the sample a careful examination of village directories of Census 2001 of both the districts from the Primary Census Abstract 2001 was done. The villages of both the districts were sorted out in the descending (decreasing) order of literacy rates. The sorting of village directories of both the districts were thought essential so that the villages with higher literacy rates were arranged at the top of the Lists while the villages with lower literacy rates were arranged at the bottom of these Lists. For this purpose, soft copies of the village-wise lists from the Primary Census Abstract 2001 in MS-Excel formats were used. As the MS-Excel formats of Primary Census Abstract 2001 present the data in absolute numbers, one column was added for depicting the literacy rates of each village for the purpose of sorting these lists. The Lists were then sorted out as per the figures in the added column. For calculating literacy rates, the standard formula (as shown below) was used.

$$\text{Literacy of Village X} = \frac{\text{No. of Literates in village X}}{\text{Population aged 7 + of village X}} \times 100$$

The details of drawing the sample are as follows:

In the first place, a total of 13 villages were selected purposively from the high literacy villages from Mansa beginning from the top of the sorted village list and moving towards the bottom of the sorted village list of this district. Thereafter another 13 villages from Mansa were purposively selected from the low literacy villages beginning from the bottom of the sorted village list and moving towards the top of the sorted village list of Mansa. This way, from Mansa, 13 villages of high literacy rates were randomly drawn from the top of the village list and 13 villages of low literacy rates were picked up from the bottom of the village list for the sample. Adopting the same top-down approach for drawing high literacy villages and bottom-up approach for the low literacy villages, 13 villages of high literacy and 13 villages of low literacy from Muktsar were also randomly drawn from the sorted village list of this district.

This procedure was thought essential under the presumption that the sample of villages so selected would provide a sufficient literacy gap between the two sets of villages which would eventually provide a better analysis, interpretation and understanding of the problem under investigation.

The selection of the villages was done with utmost care. Only that village was picked up which fulfilled the required criterion (shown below). Apart from the literacy figures, some additional aspects were also taken into account while selecting a village (and thereby the school and the VEDC). The details are as follows:

1. The village having a reasonably good number of households (at least 150) with at least one primary school. This was considered essential to have a better understanding of the dynamics of community participation in the management of the specific school.
2. To have a better analysis and interpretation of the problem under investigation, the VEDCs perceived as reasonably good (by the Education Department officials like the Block Resource Persons (BRPs), Cluster Resource Persons (CRPs) and the District Resource Persons (DRPs) have been purposively chosen for the Sample.
3. In order to ensure reliable, valid and systematic collection of essential data, only those VEDCs were identified which were formed after the June 2003 Panchayat elections and before the May 2008 Panchayat elections.

Finally a total of 411 members of the VEDCs and 99 school teachers constituted the sample for the present study. The members of the VEDCs comprised of Head Teachers, Panchayat members, members of the PTA, Ex-servicemen, Retired teacher and Philanthropist/NRIs. All the members of the 52 VEDCs selected for the sample (26 VEDCs from Mansa and 26 VEDCs Muktsar) were interviewed. As a VEDC usually has 08 members, a total of 416 VEDC members were initially planned to be interviewed. However, 05 VEDCs members could not be interviewed due to death, unavailability and unwillingness of these members. Thus the final sample consisted of 411 VEDCs members (206 from district Mansa and 205 from district Muktsar).

From the selected 52 Rural Primary schools (26 Rural Primary schools from Mansa 26 rural Primary schools from Muktsar, 02 teachers from each school were random chosen and interviewed. Though, this sample has to be 104 but 05 teachers could not interviewed due to unwillingness and unavailability (vacancy). This way, the sample consisted of 99 teachers (49 teachers from Mansa and 50 teachers from Muktsar).

Table 6.1: Sample of Villages (thereby the Schools and VEDCs)

Literacy	*Mansa*	*Muktsar*	*Both Districts*
High literacy	13	13	26
Low literacy	13	13	26
Total	26	26	52
Sample of VEDC Members			
High literacy	104	104	208
Low literacy	102	101	203
Total	206	205	411
Sample of Teachers			
High literacy	26	26	52
Low literacy	23	24	47
Total	49	50	99

The Composition, Formation and Functions of the Village Education Development Committee

This section aims at studying the composition, formation and functions of the Village Education Development Committees in the State. To achieve this objective, the relevant information has been gathered primarily from the secondary sources particularly the guidelines prepared by the Sarva Shiksha Abhiyan Authority,

Table 6.2: Sample of VEDCs members segregated as per Positions

VEDCs Members (Position-wise)	*District Mansa*			*District Muktsar*			*Total*
	High Literacy Villages (13)	*Low Literacy Villages (13)*	*Total Villages (26)*	*High Literacy Villages (13)*	*Low Literacy Villages (13)*	*Total Villages (26)*	*(N=52)*
Head Teachers	13	13	26	13	13	26	52
Panchayat Members	26	26	52	26	25	51	103
PTA Members	26	25	51	26	25	51	102
Ex-Servicemen	13	13	26	13	13	26	52
Retired Teachers	13	12	25	13	13	26	51
Philanthropists/NRIs	13	13	26	13	12	25	51
Total	104	102	206	104	101	205	411

Government of Punjab and the circulars and orders issued in this regard by the appropriate government authorities from time to time. The functions of VEDCs as perceived by its members have also been tabulated and analyzed in a separate section.

The Composition

It is mandatory for a Village Education Development Committee to have eight members. Two members have to be from the village panchayat, two from the Parent Teacher Association (PTA), one member each has to be ex-military personnel, a philanthropist/ NRI and a retired teacher of the Government of Punjab. The head teacher of the concerned school is the secretary of the VEDC. The guidelines make it mandatory that out of the two members from village panchayat at least one has to be a woman and so also from among the two PTA members, atleast one member essentially has to be a woman. Thus, as per the government guidelines, it is essential for a VEDC to have atleast two women members.

However, the composition of VEDCs in the State of Punjab has been amended in the year 2010. Under the new guidelines, there has to be three ex-officio members namely the school head master/principal, senior school teacher and an anganwadi worker. Apart from the ex-officio members, there has to be eight non-official members namely two members of local panchayat (at least one to be a female), two Parent Teacher Association (PTA) members (at least one to be a female), one ex-serviceman, one retired teacher, one philanthropist/NRI and mother/father of a disabled child (6-14 years). The school head master/principal acts as member secretary of VEDC. For the present study since only those VEDCs have been studied which were formed after the June 2003 Panchayat elections and before the May 2008 Panchayat elections, the study takes into account the Government guidelines which were in place during that period (2003-2008). The study found that the guidelines of the government are strictly adhered as far as the composition of VEDC is concerned. It is primarily because the VEDC is under the overall control of the DEO (Primary) and all the nominations of VEDC members are to be finally approved by the DEO (Primary). She/he is solely responsible for the smooth functioning of this body.

The Process of Formation

The Village Education Development Committees are formed by the process of nomination at various levels except that the Chairman can be elected. As per the guidelines of the Sarva Shiksha Abhiyan Authority, Government of Punjab, the formation of the VEDC is the responsibility of the DEO (Elementary Education). Nomination of the members of the VEDC is done at various levels. The village panchayat pass a resolution and nominate two of the members of panchayat to the VEDC. Similarly the PTA of the school nominates two members to this committee. The nomination of ex-serviceman as the member of the VEDC is also done by the PTA whereas, the rest of the members are nominated by the DEO (Primary) on the recommendations of the head teacher of the school. The Chairman of VEDC is elected by the members only if there is no consensus among the members on any one. The head teacher, however, is not eligible to vote as a member in the election of the chairman of the VEDC.

After receiving all the nominations, the DEO (Elementary Education) constitute the VEDC. The VEDCs have three years' tenure. Any change or substitution of VEDC members is done by the DEO (Elementary Education) only as he is solely responsible for the smooth functioning of the VEDC and the VEDC is under the overall control of the DEO (Elementary Education).

The tenure of the VEDC members nominated by the PTA ends with the cessation of their PTA membership. In case of a vacancy of a PTA member, a new member has to be nominated by the PTA and approved by the DEO (Elementary Education). In case, the ex-serviceman leaves the village permanently or is not available due to whatever reasons, then the VEDC, by passing a resolution, makes a request to the PTA to nominate a new ex-serviceman from the village to the VEDC. Similarly, if the retired teacher is not available due to whatever reasons, then the VEDC will pass a resolution and nominate any other retired government employee of some other department as the VEDC member. Thereafter the VEDC will recommend his/her name for approval to the DEO (Elementary Education).

In the event of any VEDC member being unavailable due to whatever reasons, the works undertaken by the VEDC has to continue and the VEDC has to pass a resolution to this effect immediately and make efforts to nominate a new member in his place as per the laid down procedure. No membership of the VEDC can remain vacant for more than three months. The DEO (Elementary Education) has to ensure that, at no stage, the number of VEDC members is less than the prescribed norms. In case of such a situation arises, the DEO (Elementary Education) is held responsible.

As per the Guidelines of the of the Sarva Shiksha Abhiyan Authority, Government of Punjab, after the completion of the term/ tenure of the panchayat, the new panchayat has to nominate the new members to the VEDC and get them approved by the DEO (Elementary Education). Although it is the DEO (Elementary Education) who has to form the next VEDC as and when required but it is expected that in the course of time, depending upon the experiences and performance, the VEDC would slowly be transformed as a Committee to be formed entirely by the village people themselves.

The norms of formation of VEDC have been slightly modified by the Sarva Shiksha Abhiyan Authority, Government of Punjab in 2010. The new guidelines mandate that the chairman of VEDC has to be elected by the majority from amongst the VEDC members other than the ex-officio members. For nominating the PRI members, the Panchayat has to pass a resolution and send to the Head teacher. The tenure of Panchayat members as the members of VEDC would be co-terminus with the tenure of the Panchayat. With the formation of new Panchayat, new nominations would be done. The nominations of the PTA members are to be done by the school PTA by passing a resolution. Only those PTA members are made the members of the VEDC whose children study in that particular school. The PTA members remain the VEDC members till such time they are members of the PTA. The responsibility of nominations of the ex-serviceman, philanthropist, retired teacher and the senior-most teacher would rest with the head master. For ex-serviceman, the highest rank and length of service is given preference. As philanthropist such person from amongst the villagers is nominated who has donated the maximum amount of money to the school. The senior-most teacher who is to be the VEDC member is from among the school staff and he/she would be excluding the head master. This teacher is also authorised to act as the secretary of VEDC in the absence the head teacher. The formation of VEDC is finally sent to DEO (Elementary Education) by the head teacher for approval. The DEO (Elementary Education) then approves the formation and sent the same back to the head teacher. The tenure of VEDC has to three years from the date of approval by the DEO (Elementary Education). The VEDC can, however, change any unfit member by passing a resolution but such a change can be made only with the approval of the DEO (Elementary Education). The present study found that all the VEDCs are formed strictly in accordance with the guidelines as laid down by the Sarva Shiksha Abhiyan Authority Punjab from time to time.

The Functions of VEDCs

The functions of the Village Education Committees vary from state to state, however, the main functions across all states, inter alia, are to work towards increasing the enrolment and reducing the number of out-of-school children, to monitor student's attendance and to check on school drop-out rates and to ensure equity in education in terms of gender, location, socio-economic deprivation or disability.

In Punjab, the VEDCs are fully authorized to take any appropriate decision in the interest of the school. As per the Government guidelines, the specific functions of VEDCs in Punjab are following:

i. The VEDCs have to consider new plans for improvement of the school and the standard of education.
ii. The VEDCs should create awareness among the community people regarding the use of utilization of funds and projects meant for school development.
iii. The VEDCs should attempt to inform the village people about the improvement plans and management processes meant for the school.
iv. The VEDCs should ensure participation of the community to the possible extent in the activities undertaken for effective functioning of the school and will mobilize volunteers towards achieving these goals.
v. VEDCS can review the progress of the work/activities undertaken for the improvement of the school and to prepare the progress report.
vi. The VEDCs have to provide full and proper information to all the stakeholders regarding ongoing developmental

activities/work undertaken by the VEDC and make efforts to solve all types of local problems of the school.

vii. The VEDCs have to motivate the children engaged in labour, their parents and the employers to send the children to school and VEDC has will monitor and motivate out-of-school children and their parents for school education.

Additional Functions

i. The VEDCs should undertake repairs and renovation of school building and will work grow trees and plants around the school building and to look after them.

ii. The VEDCs make arrangements for basic facilities like water, electricity, open air, light and fans etc. and the black board, make purchases of the furniture and ensure their proper upkeep care.

iii. The VEDCs maintain cleanliness and sanitation in and around the school and ensure beautification and development of the area around the school.

iv. The VEDCs make arrangements for playgrounds in the school and ensure their proper upkeep and maintenance.

v. The VEDCs provide help in the academic work of the school like procurement of Teaching Learning Material (TLM) etc. and make arrangements for the school library and ensure the availability of newspapers and magazines etc essential for intellectual development of children.

vi. The VEDCs make arrangements for sports material to the students and organize sports competitions for them and to arrange/organize educational tours for the students and organize cultural programmes in the school and make arrangements for recreational facilities for the students.

vii. The VEDCs organize intellectual, social, academic and physical activities essential for overall development of the children.

viii. The VEDCs make arrangements for medicines and first aids for students during emergency and to provide help to the students in need.

ix. The VEDCs have to work for enrolling the out of school children in school and prepare the list of children who are enrolled and who are not-enrolled and will monitor and ensure the timely distribution of scholarships, textbooks etc. to Scheduled Caste, handicap and girl students.

x. The VEDCs have to attend and address the personal problems of the children of the poorer families and from lower castes and ensure that these children go to school.

xi. The VEDCs have to maintain discipline in the school in such a way that the process of learning is not hindered and the children have a joyful experience.

xii. The VEDCs have to initiate and undertake other appropriate activities aimed at development and growth of the school and the students and will work towards fulfillment of educational needs of the school.

The Sarva Shiksha Abhiyan Authority Punjab has made significant modifications in the functions in its guidelines published in 2010. The major functions of the VEDCs as per the latest guidelines are following:

i. The VEDCs should identify every child in the age group of 6-14 years and would see whether or not all the children in the village are going to school.

ii. The VEDCs are to find out the reasons why children do not go to the school, in case; there are out-of-school children in the village.

iii. The VEDCs should establish contact with the parents of out-of-school children and ensure that these children are enrolled in the school.

iv. The VEDCs are expected to make efforts to solve the problems of the school and bring the issue in the notice of the higher authorities and work to eliminate the deficiencies in the school through conciliation.

v. The VEDCs are expected to enlighten children about the prevalence of social evils and their consequences and make everyone aware about the mission of Sarva Shiksha Abhiyan.

vi. The VEDCs are expected to initiate special drives for girls' education and ensure that the children with special needs receive all the incentives given to them under Sarva Shiksha Abhiyan.

vii. The VEDCs can initiate discussion on quality of school education in all Gram Sabha meetings and monitor the school systems.

viii. The VEDCs should take care of the availability of drinking water, electricity, fresh air, light, fans and black boards in the school and ensure proper arrangements for the Mid Day Meals in the school.

ix. The VEDCs have to take care of the cleanliness in and around the school and particularly the school toilets.

x. The VEDCs are expected to initiate need-based programmes for all round development of the children as well as the school.

xi. The VEDCs should keep a watch on the grants received the school from time to time and ensure that every grant is spent as per rules and proper account of their utilization is maintained.

xii. The VEDCs have to ensure discipline in the school in such a way that alongside the academic work, the children will have a joyful learning is the school.

Functions of VEDCs as Stated by the Members

In order to study the functions of the VEDCs, the members were also asked about the functions of the VEDCs as perceived by them as a member of these committees. The responses of these members show that for majority members (76.4%), the main function of VEDCs is to undertake civil/construction and maintenance work in the school while more than two-fifth (42.3%) members were of the view that the VEDCs have to assist in proper utilization of grants/funds received from the government from time to time for the development of the school. An almost equal proportion (40.4%) of the VEDCs members was of the opinion that the major function of these committees is to identify the needs and problems of the school. Other functions as stated by these respondents were to organize functions and celebrations in the schools (25.3%), to monitor performance of children, attendance and quality of education (23.6%), to inform higher authorities about the problems of school and teachers (22.1%) and to ensure that the teachers come on time and take class (20.9%).

From the views of the members, it is clear that the VEDCs

mainly focus on issues that involve money like the civil works and utilization of grants. Other functions as mandated in the Guidelines are not given much attention in the day to day working of these bodies. Although the VEDCs have been entrusted to undertake a wide spectrum of functions which cover almost every aspect of the management of village school but there remains a wide gap when it comes to the actual implementation of all these functions. The data makes it clear that there are many functions of VEDCs that are not even known to the members of these bodies what to talk of their implementation. The awareness of VEDCs members about functions, composition and formation has been discussed in details in a subsequent section of this chapter.

The Socio-Demographic Profile

This section presents the information on the socio-demographic profile of VEDC members in terms of gender, age, education, caste and marital status. These indicators have been analyzed from the field data. For this purpose, a total of 411 VEDCs members were interviewed from 52 purposively selected VEDCs (26 VEDCs from Mansa District and 26 VEDCs from Muktsar District). The examination of the socio-demographic profile of VEDC members was thought essential because of the well established fact that in a society as diverse as this, the factors such as gender, age, education, religion, caste and marital status play an important role towards involvement in the decision making processes as well as in performance of duties and functions as assigned in various aspects of an individual's life. Against the foregoing arguments, it is assumed that the socio-demographic profile of members of VEDCs is an important aspect in order to determine their entry and involvement in these committees.

Gender

Gender is a social construct that not only manifests the ascribed status and style of life but also determine the nature and pattern of involvement of an individual in his/her day to day activities. In ascription-oriented societies such as this, the gender plays an important role in discharging the social responsibilities assigned to us in our daily life (Rani: 2002). Considering this viewpoint, the study attempts to know the gender of the VEDCs members so as to understand the role of gender in the initial entry or nomination of these members to the VEDC.

As has been pointed out earlier, it is mandatory for a VEDC to have at least two women members, one each from the two panchayat members and two PTA members. The analysis of the data shows that the membership of the women to the VEDCs was bare minimum. In all the VEDCs, the number of women was only upto the extent to which it met the mandatory requirement of the Government Guidelines. It is clear from the data that out of the total respondents, 29.4 per cent were female while the rest (70.6%) were male members. This percentage is marginally higher than the mandated proportion of 25 per cent prescribed in the Government Guidelines for women membership to the VEDCs. The higher margin than the prescribed 25 per cent is not because of the women members nominated to the VEDCs but it is due to the presence of female head teachers who are ex-officio members to these committees. It is worthwhile to mention that the government guidelines prescribes only the lower limit of 25 per cent for women membership whereas there is no upper limit as prescribed under the norms. Thus the upper limit of women membership to VEDCs can be as high as even 100 per cent. But it was sad to note that there was no VEDC in the sample wherein the women membership was found to be higher than the minimum prescribed number. The findings corroborate the conclusions of the study carried out by Narayana and Chandrakant (2000) who finds that there was no proper representation of women in VECs in Maharashtra.

From the analysis, it can be concluded the entry of women into VEDCs is mainly due to the mandatory provision of having at least two women as VEDC members provided in the government guidelines. The VEDCs, by and large, remain a male bastion and the personal merit of woman remains overshadowed by the patriarchal stereotypes and culture factors adverse to gender equality. This aspect is reinforced by Menon (1999) who concludes that women in VECs in Haryana observed *purdah* and many of them didn't even looked upto male members and speak in the meetings due to cultural reasons. Regional variations on this aspect were not very pronounced.

Age

It is a well established fact that age serves as an index of an individual's experience, awareness and wisdom in general. Traditionally age is considered an important factor in respect to one's status and prestige, particularly in rural societies and as such the older people are given privilege to occupy key positions in the village. (Bhargava: 1979). Age is quite significant to an individual for whom both experience and maturity are essential in role performance (Bhargava: 1979). At the same time, it is also true that in the modern day development context, it is believed and has been proved that the young and energetic people are on increase in the leadership positions particularly in local self government institutions (Singh: 1985). Against these two opposite view points, it has been attempted in the present analysis to identify what sort of situation prevailed in the VEDCs with respect to the age of the members of this local school governance body. The analysis indicated that the VEDCs in Punjab continue to be dominated by the not so young people. It was noted from the analysis that 45.3 per cent respondents were in the age group of 45-60 years and 18.7 per cent respondents were in the age group of 60 years and above. This clearly indicates that 64 per cent VEDCs members were older than 45 years of age. On the other hand, about one-third (33.1%) respondents were in younger age group of 30-45 years while just about 2.9 per cent were in between 18 and 30 years of age.

The findings establish the fact that the older people continue to outnumber the younger people as far as the participation in the school related issues is concerned. The survey clearly indicates that age still remains an important criterion in determining the leadership positions in rural areas particularly when it comes to participation in the school related activities. These conclusions are substantiating by Singh (1985) who in his study highlights that rural leadership still continues to be dominated by the aged.

Two reasons can be attributed to the phenomenon of relatively older persons being nominated to the VEDCs. First, it may be due to the composition of the VEDCs itself as out of the total VEDCs members, the retired teachers, the philanthropists/NRIs, Ex-servicemen and the head teachers are usually from the older age groups. The analysis corroborate the foregoing arguments as among the retired teachers, 86.2 per cent were more than 60 years of age while in case of Ex-servicemen, more than three-fifth (61.5%) were between 45 and 60 years of age. Similarly more than two-fifth (43.1%) philanthropists/NRIs were in the age group of 45-60 years and about one-fifth (19.6%) of them were more than 60 years. As regards the head teachers nearly three-fifth (59.6%) of them were between 45 and 60 years of age.

The second reason for this trend could be the fact that the membership to VEDCs is determined by nominations and not by elections where age is likely to play a greater role than other personality attributes of an individual, primarily because in rural societies, the age is still considered as a defining factor of respect and dignity of an individual and thus relatively older people get preference over the youngsters when it comes to determining the membership of the VEDCs through nominations. Therefore the elder persons stand better chances of getting nominating to the VEDCs in comparison the younger people.

From the findings, it can be concluded that the age of a person still holds the key to the determination of membership to the Village Education Development Committees in the area of the present study.

Level of Education

Education provides the fundamental basis for effective participation of people in the process of development of any society. It plays an important role in all aspects of an individual's daily life. Education essentially is a pre-requisite for any individual or a community to have a better quality of life (Nayak: 2009). At the community level, education is important to make people aware of their rights and duties and help them fruitfully participate in social, economic and educational activities. Since the present study primarily focuses on the community participation in school education through Village Education Development Committees, it is important to know the education levels of the VEDCs members. The knowledge of the level of education of these members is all the more important because their education would ultimately impinge on the quality and the extent of their participation in the school related activities. The education would provide them the acquisition of new skills and abilities eventually promoting overall human development. (Rao: 2008). It is in this context that the educational background of the members of the VEDCs has been studied under present investigation. For this purpose the respondents have been classified into six educational categories namely illiterate, respondents who had studied up to primary level, secondary and higher secondary levels, graduation and post graduation levels. It is evident from the analysis that out of the total 411 respondents, just 08 (1.9%) were illiterate while the rest of them had formal education ranging from primary level to post graduation level. It is observed that 28.7 per cent VEDCs members were graduates while 10 per cent were post graduate which means that a little less than two-fifth (38.7%) of the members of the VEDCs had acquired higher education. The analysis further shows that nearly one-fourth (22.6%) of them had passed higher secondary while 29.7 per cent were matriculates. This means that the VEDCs members were fairly educated as more than 90 per cent of the total members had formal educational qualifications higher than matriculation level. The findings are also corroborated by the study done by the Karnataka Government (2004) in collaboration with Azim Premji Foundation which found that 90 per cent of the presidents in the School Development and Management Committees in the State were educated.

Castes/Category

Caste system is most peculiar feature of the rural communities in India. Caste occupies a crucial significance in the day to day activities of the village life. In traditional rural societies, leadership roles were performed mainly by the higher castes (Srinivas: 1959). In modern times also, the caste issues greatly influence the mechanism for community participation in all aspects particularly the education related matters. The caste in Indian society determines the status, the functions and the roles of individuals and groups to a large extent. It affects the way the rural community interacts with each other (Nayak: 2009). In this context, the data on caste/category of the members of the VEDCs was considered vital to understand the dynamics of community participation in school related issues. For a better analysis, the respondents have been broadly divided into three major groups namely the general castes, other backward castes and the scheduled castes categories.

It is apparent from the analysis that nearly three-fifth (59.4%) members belonged to general castes followed by the scheduled castes (31.1%). Nearly one-tenth (9.5%) members belonged to the other backward castes groups. The proportion of the scheduled castes members was much less than the general castes members. The trends in the higher literacy villages were similar to that of low literacy villages; however, the proportion of general castes was slightly higher (62.1%) in the low literacy villages in comparison to the high literacy villages (56.7%).

As regards the scheduled castes, the percentage was slightly higher (33.7%) in high literacy villages than the low literacy villages (28.6%). From the analysis it is clear that the VEDCs are primarily dominated by the people from the general castes. This is mainly because of the absence of caste-based provisions of reservation for VEDC memberships in the guidelines of the State government. Though the Guidelines mentions that there must be reasonable representation of all the castes residing in a village community, the people of dominant castes continue to form the bulk of leadership positions in rural areas, at least, as far as the membership to VEDCs is concerned. These arguments find support from Tyagi (1999) who is of the view of that influential and powerful people want to see themselves or their favourites as VECs members. In the light of the above, it is concluded that in absence of specific reservation provisions, the people of dominant castes tend to monopolize the leadership positions at the village level particularly with reference to community participation in the school related activities.

Marital Status

Marriage is one of the social institutions which always have been accorded immense respect and recognition in any society. It is regarded as most sacred and an institution that not only enlarges the social boundaries of the married person but also acts as an extension of his/her social relations and responsibilities (Kapadia: 1966). In the process of achieving leadership roles as is the membership to VEDCs, the marital status of an individual certainly plays its own contribution in enlarging the support-base as well as in gaining acceptance from the community members. Against this backdrop the analysis of the marital status of the members of the VEDCs is pertinent in relation to the determination of their nomination as a member of the VEDC in the community.

From the data, it is apparent that a huge majority (97.3%) of the VEDC members were married while only a few (2.7%) were unmarried. The findings thus reinforce the argument that the marital status of an individual certainly has a positive role in the process of acquiring leadership roles like the membership to a Village Education Development Committee at the community level. This, however, may not be interpreted as saying that the unmarried person in anyway are at a disadvantage and denied leadership roles but none the less it is amply clear from the data that the marriage as an institution certainly provides an enlarged social space to an individual in the rural communities. The present claims are in corroboration of that to Kapadia (1966) who argues that the institution of marriage enlarges the social boundary of an individual.

The Awareness of the Members

This section aims at having an understanding about the awareness of the members of the Village Education Development Committees about the composition, process of formation and functions of these bodies in the light of fourth objective of the study. It is because awareness, as such, is one of the important variables for meaningful participation in any committee such as the VEDC. An inquiry into the awareness of the members was thought essential under the assumption that well informed members are likely to perform their roles as a VEDC member in a far better way. In order to establish as to what actually the VEDCs members know about various aspects of the functioning of these bodies, the present analysis was done. For the sake of clarity, the analysis has been done across the head teachers, panchayat and PTA members, retired teachers, ex-servicemen and the philanthropists/NRIs.

Awareness about Composition of VEDCs

As pointed out earlier that as per the government guidelines (unrevised), the Village Education Development Committees comprises of eight members, out of whom, two are from village panchayat with at least one female whereas another two are from the PTA (with at least one female). Besides, one member each is a retired teacher, an ex-serviceman and a philanthropist/NRI. The head teacher of the school is the member secretary of the VEDC. The Guidelines were slightly revised in the year 2010. The present analysis takes into account the unrevised guidelines (prior to the year 2010) because when the data was collected in 2008-09, the unrevised guidelines were in place. The analysis in the present section has been done on a three point scale-fully aware, somewhat aware and not at all aware. It revealed that there were only 5.1 per cent respondents in the sample who replied that they were not at all aware about the composition of the VEDC while about one-third (32.1%) respondents stated to be fully aware about it. A huge chunk of more than three fifth (62.8%) respondents were in the middle category i.e. they were neither absolutely ignorant about the composition nor were they fully aware about the composition of the VEDCs. The investigation further revealed that the respondents in the middle category were well educated and seemingly aware about the composition of this body but they lacked the confidence to take the risk of saying that they know it all. Overall, the awareness of the VEDCs members about the composition of the body was fairly good. There was not much difference across the high and low literacy regions.

During the course of field work, it was observed that head teachers were the most informed members among all the respondents. This was most obvious because it is the head teacher who has the ultimate responsibility for the overall functioning of the VEDCs. It is he who has to maintain each and every record of this body and he is the one who is directly answerable to the higher authorities for all aspects of its working in the capacity of member secretary of VEDC. The analysis revealed that all the head teachers in the sample said to have been fully aware about the composition of the VEDCs. As regards the panchayat members, more than half (52.4%) were knowing all about the composition of VEDC while 5.8 per cent of them were totally ignorant about it. The awareness level of the members of the PTA was relatively low as only 8.8 per cent of them expressed that they were fully aware while a great majority (83.3%) were in the intermediary category. In case of ex-military personnel, the proportion of fully aware category was 11.5 per cent while not at all aware category was 3.8 per cent. Contrary to the expectations, the retired teachers did not seem to be very well aware about the composition as it is evident from the data that only a little more than one tenth (11.8%) of them stated to be fully aware while 84.3 per cent of them replied that they were only partially aware about the exact requirements for the composition of this body. The survey further showed that only 9.8 per cent philanthropists/NRIs were fully aware while 84.3 per cent were partially aware and 5.9 per cent were totally ignorant about the composition of VEDCs. The regional variations on this aspect of the VEDC were not very pronounced.

From these findings, it can be concluded that the awareness of VEDCs members to an extent of 32.1 per cent being fully aware while 62.8 per cent being partially aware present a fairly good scenario. However, it does not mean to conclude that there is no scope for improvement. The awareness (thereby the performance) of the members of VEDCs can further be improved by providing regular periodic trainings to the members on this aspect. The respondents who are in the middle category of awareness can certainly be made to cross over to the first category provided they are given proper knowledge inputs by way of organizing some lecture/seminar/workshops etc. at the school level. This definitely is not something which is unachievable and unrealistic. The member secretaries and the chairpersons themselves can organize such an event on awareness generation in their respective schools.

Awareness about Process of Formation of VEDCs

As has been pointed out earlier, the membership to VEDCs is determined by nominations as per the guidelines prescribed by the government in this regard. The main responsibility for formation of VEDC lies on the DEO (elementary education). The VEDC members from the panchayats are nominated by the village panchayat itself by passing a resolution to this effect. Similarly the PTA of the school nominates two members from amongst themselves and sends them to this Committee. The nomination of the ex-serviceman is also done by the PTA. The names of the retired teacher and the philanthropist/NRI are recommended by the head teacher to the DEO (elementary) for the approval of nomination to this Body. After all the nominations, it is the responsibility of the DEO (elementary) to constitute the VEDC for a period of three years. Any subsequent change/modification or substitution of the membership can be done only with the prior approval of the DEO (elementary). The analysis shows that the membership to the VEDCs is done through nominations, however, the chairman may be elected, in case; there is no consensus on any member. The elections can be held only in rare cases where chances of agreement are remote. The survey revealed that all the village Education Development Committees in the State are formed strictly as per the guidelines laid down by the government.

As regards the awareness regarding the process of formation, the data reflects that about 17.3 per cent of the members of the VEDC did not know anything about the procedure followed for nominating various members i.e. who nominates whom etc. These respondents did not seem to be interested as well in knowing about the procedures as VEDCs were not on their priority list. They held the membership of VEDC just for the sake of paper formalities. Interestingly many of them were those whose children were studying in private schools. The observation revealed that the ignorance was more because of the lack of intention of the members than the lack of education. On the other side of the awareness scale, a little less than one-third (29.0%) respondents were fully aware about the process of formation of VEDCs.

Among them were all the head teachers and the chairmen of the VEDCs. Awareness of members (excluding secretaries and chairpersons) was very less (6.5%). The regional variations in this regard were not very pronounced as there were no marked differences between the percentages across the low and high literacy regions and so also across Mansa and Muktsar. Further break-up of the data shows that it was the PTA members among the VEDCs members whose proportion was the highest (28.4%) as far as the extent of ignorance about the formation of VEDCs is concerned. It was evident from the data that a little less than one-third(28.4%) PTA members stated to have been 'not at all' aware followed by the philanthropist/NRI (25.5%) and the ex-servicemen (19.2%). From the data it is also clear that among the panchayat members, 45.6 per cent replied to be fully aware where as the proportion of PTA members and the philanthropists/NRIs was only 9.8 per cent while for the retired teachers, the proportion was 7.8 per cent.

From the analysis, it can be suggested that there is a possibility of sharing more information with the VEDCs members on the procedures followed for formation of this Committee. As majority of the members were in the middle category of awareness scale i.e. partially aware, it underlines the urgency of motivating this chunk so as to enable them to cross over to the fully aware category of awareness. The information sharing coupled with motivation can possibly lead to more involvement of the members in the school related activities, thereby, improving the functioning of the committees and the standards of school education at the village level.

Awareness about Determination of Membership of VEDCs

As has been pointed out in the preceding section, the members to the VEDCs are appointed by the process of nomination at various levels. The elections can be held only in case, there is no consensus on any member and particularly with reference to the chairperson of the VEDCs. In order to know the awareness level of the VEDC on this aspect, the respondents were specifically asked whether the membership to VEDCs is determined by nomination or election and who is the nominating authority for various categories of the VEDCs members. The responses solicited from the respondents have been analyzed and presented in Tabular form. From the data, it was found that maximum respondents (72.5%) expressed the views that the members to the VEDC are nominated rather than elected. There were just 2.7 per cent respondents who replied that the membership is determined through elections.

Here it may be pointed out that although the nomination is the preferred mode of determining the membership to VEDCs, however, elections can also be held in case there is lack of consensus on a particular candidate. Further the data depicted that a little less than one fourth (24.8%) respondents expressed ignorance as to how an individual made a member of this committee. Besides all the head teachers, a great majority of panchayat members (87.4%) and the retired teachers (86.3%) were knowing that the membership to VEDC is determined by nominations. The proportion of philanthropists/NRIs was 60.8 per cent while the ex-servicemen was 55.8 per cent. The proportion of PTA members was 51 per cent on this aspect.

In answer to the second query as who nominates whom, the data reveals that nearly three-fifth (59.6%) respondents knew that the panchayat members are nominated by village panchayat, 68.6 per cent knew that the PTA members are nominated by the PTA. The PTA also nominates the retired teacher was replied correctly by 66.7 per cent respondents. 34.8 per cent respondents knew that philanthropist/NRI is nominated by the DEO (Elementary Education) on recommendations from the head teacher. It can be inferred from the data that although the respondents were reasonably aware about the fact that the nominations is the principle criterion for determination of membership, however, the awareness on as to who nominate whom was relatively less. Saying more generally, the actual procedure adopted for determining the membership was not very well known by the members. Thus, the findings were in conformity to the general perception that the specifics of the nominations to the VEDCs are not very precisely known to the VEDCs members. As regards the regional variations, no marked difference was apparent across the high and low literacy regions.

Awareness about Functions of VEDCs

The specific functions of the Village Education Development Committees in the state of Punjab have been discussed in the preceding sections. The present section is devoted only to know the extent of awareness among the VEDCs members about these functions. The level of awareness of the members have been analysed on a three-point scale namely: fully aware, somewhat aware and not at all aware. The respondents were also asked to list the functions of VEDCs as perceived by them in their day to day working as a member of this committee.

More generally, the functions of VEDCs are to initiate and undertake all appropriate activities aimed at the improvement of the village school and to work towards fulfillment of educational needs of the community. These activities may include undertaking repairs and renovation of school infrastructure, organizing intellectual, social and physical activities, creating awareness and ensuring community involvement and so on. From the analysis, it was evident that about three fourth of the respondents were not fully aware as to what are the specific functions of the VEDCs. The discussions during the course of field work revealed that the respondents have not even read the literature available in schools about the functions of this body. For majority (76.4%) of the respondents, the major functions of the VEDC are to undertake civil/construction works in the schools.

The analysis depicted that the awareness of VEDCs members about functions of VEDCs was very less. The findings are in conformity of the conclusions of the study carried out by Institute of Rural Research and Development (2010) according to which more than half of the VEC members in Haryana were inadequately informed about their roles and responsibilities. The findings by Lal (1997) also reinforce these claims as he finds that the awareness level of members of School Management Committees in Bihar about the functions of SMCs was below average. Overall in the present study, only a little more than one-fourth (25.8%) respondents replied that they knew all about the functions of this body. The findings suggested that the members of the VEDCs needed more information on the functions of VEDCs. This can be done through periodic trainings or awareness lectures by appropriate officials of the Government. The members mainly perceived VEDCs as the bodies meant to undertake the construction/civil works and for carrying out activities relating to the utilization of grants or organizing social functions/celebrations at the school level. Here lies the scope of changing this perception that the VEDCs are the people' forum made to encourage community participation in school activities so as to improve the quality of educational services at the village level by performing functions of a varied nature and not just the functions relating to the utilization of grants/funds and organizing the cultural programmes. Ironically, no member (except Secretaries) perceived VEDCs as a community owned institution made to achieve better standards of school education at the grassroots level.

Summing Up

From the foregoing analysis it clear that the VEDCs in the State of Punjab are formed strictly according to the norms set out by the Government. The functions of the VEDCs cover almost every aspect of the management of school, however, the committees don't exercise all the functions bestowed on them neither do the members know about these functions in entirety. As regards the data on the socio-demographic profile of the VEDCs members in terms of age, gender, education and caste, it is revealed that the VEDCs, by and large, remain a male bastion with majority and dominance of the rich and powerful families of the higher castes. The awareness of members of VEDCs about composition, process of formation and the functions of VEDC did not reveal an inspiring scenario. Most of the members were not aware about the nuances of the day to day working of the Village Education Committees and required constant training and education in this regard.

7

Village Education Development Committees: Slithering towards the Sunshine

Punjab is considered to be one of those states in the country whose school infrastructure is reasonably good. In fact, as per the Educational Development Index (EDI) 2011 prepared by National University of Educational Planning and Administration (NUEPA), Punjab is at the top in infrastructural parameters in the country followed by Pondicherry and Andaman and Nicobar Islands. The EDI reflects remarkable gains made by Punjab on parameters of school accessibility, infrastructure and teaching facility outcomes. The present chapter is devoted to present an overview of the general facilities available in the sampled schools apart from examining the contribution of Village Education Development Committees in the promotion of elementary education in terms of increase in enrollment, reduction in school drop-out rate, improvement in school result, contribution of members in individual capacity and conduct of meetings. The section also takes an account of the activities undertaken for improving the existing physical/infrastructural facilities, fundraising and incentives to students. This chapter further provides the problems encountered by the Village Education Development Committees and suggestions as furnished by the members towards improvement in these bodies long with the views of the teachers about the working of the Village Education Development Committees in Punjab.

The data from District Information System on Education (DISE: 2009-10) reveals that in Punjab 98 per cent habitations are covered by a primary school. There is just 2.9 per cent single classroom schools where as average number of classrooms in

2009-10 was 3.6. No school in the State is housed in *Kucha* buildings (Juyal *et al.*: 2007). On the whole, the overall situation is relatively better than many other Indian States. In the light of the above, it is being emphasized that though the State has achieved a considerable success in terms of school infrastructure but as regards the quality, upkeep, community ownership and the parity with the private schools, a lot more is required to be done. There is a stark difference between the institutional facilities available in the private schools and the government schools. The situation of private schools in terms of institutional as well as human factors such as teachers' attitude, commitment etc is very different than the government schools. There is urgency for the Government to augment the focus on institutional factors with the human factors like the attitudes and the commitment of the school teachers and parents. The experiences have shown that inspite of good service conditions and job security, the teachers of government schools don't exhibit a sense of ownership and commitment towards the upkeep and maintenance of the village schools. The parents, by and large, too have a sense of alienation towards the schools owned by the government. It is high time that the policy makers in the government must now realize that so long as the teacher and the parents, who are the central cog in the educational apparatus of the government, do not own the village school, mere availability of facilities would possibly not yield the desired educational outcomes at the community level. Against this backdrop, the subsequent sections are devoted to analyze the availability of facilities in the schools chosen for the present study. The sections provide information on the availability of various facilities in the school namely the drinking water, separate toilets for girls, electricity, availability of furniture for teachers and students, the condition of school building and other basic facilities like the boundary wall, playground, library and computers etc.

This analysis is important because all these facilities have a direct bearing on the standard of education as well as on the overall academic environment of the school. For this purpose, a separate school information questionnaire was designed to collect the required data from 52 schools drawn for the sample. The school facilities have been analyzed under four broad headings as given below:

a) Condition of building
b) Availability of drinking water, girls' toilet and electricity
c) Availability of furniture for teachers and students
d) Availability of miscellaneous facilities

Condition of School Building

As regards the school building, the data depicts that there was no school in the sample without a building or a school housed in a *kucha* building. All the school buildings were owned by the government and nearly 90 per cent school buildings were in a fairly good condition, but very poorly maintained in the sense that they were not properly white-washed or painted on regular basis. The analysis reflected that about 17.3 per cent school buildings did not need any repair whereas significantly three-fifth (75%) school buildings required one or the other repair work. For instance, some buildings required immediate white washing and painting. Some required mason work here and there. In some cases doors and windows were broken, there were no latches while in other cases ventilators required repairs and so did the electric fittings. But overall condition of these buildings was habitable and as such there was no danger to life of the students and teachers. On the other hand, 7.7 per cent school buildings needed immediate attention as they required major repairs. Although these buildings were being used for classes but the poor condition of such buildings definitely has its own adverse affect on the overall academic environment of the school. For Instance, one of the school buildings was very old with seepage and the leaking roof. Another school building was very low lying and prone to frequent water logging particularity during the rainy season. In another school, space was a big constraint for the students. The provisions for Sun light were not adequate. In another case, the pot holes in the floors of the classrooms and verandah required immediate masonry work. The observation revealed that the teachers did not seem very happy about the lengthy procedural requirements and an avoidable load of paper work involved in getting the civil works initiated and implemented in the schools and nor there was any specialized staff to work out the costs and the estimates about the civil and construction works.

The present analysis is indicative of the fact that the overall condition of the school buildings was reasonably good as there was no school whose building was found to be dilapidated and nor was any school whose building paused a danger to the life of the teachers and the students. However, these buildings required maintenance and further improvement. The VEDCs along with the State government can certainly play an important role in proper maintenance and upkeep of the school buildings in these villages.

Availability of Drinking Water, Girls' Toilet and Electricity

Availability of drinking water and toilet is one of the basic requirements in any institution such as a school. Studies have proved that there is a direct correlation between the enrollments and drop out of students and the availability of the sanitation facilities within the school premises. Sarva Shiksha Abhiyan lays a great emphasis on provisioning of the basic facilities particularly the toilets and drinking water in all schools. Under SSA, there is a convergence with other government schemes so as to achieve 100 per cent coverage of these facilities. The Department of Drinking Water Supply in the Minister of Rural Development, Government of India has got provisions under Accelerated Rural Water Supply Programme to cover all rural schools with drinking water facility. The Total Sanitation Campaign (TSC) provides toilets and urinals for rural schools in coordination with local Panchayati Raj Institutions (MHRD: 2008). With these efforts and the efforts of many civil society organizations, a considerable success has been achieved towards provisioning the services relating to drinking water and sanitation in village schools. According to DISE (2009-10), 99.45 per cent schools in Punjab have drinking water facilities while 99.02 per cent schools had girls' toilets. According to the study carried out by Singh (2007) all primary schools in District Mansa had drinking water facilities where as there was a separate toilet for girls in 88.89 per cent rural primary schools in Mansa district. Similarly all the primary schools in rural areas in District Muktsar had drinking water as well as separate toilets for girls (Singh and Choudhary: 2007). The present study finds that all schools in District Muktsar and Mansa had drinking water facilities whereas 96.2 per cent schools in Mansa and 100 per cent schools of District Muktsar had girls' toilets. In total 98.1 per cent schools in the sample had girls' toilets within the school premises.

Thus it can be concluded from the analysis that the efforts under Sarva Shiksha Abhiyan and other schemes of the government are making a discernible impact on the quality of school infrastructure at the village level. The role of VEDCs in creating school infrastructure is discussed at length in a subsequent chapter.

As regards the availability of a proper electricity connection in the school, the analysis revealed that there were a little more than one-third (36.5%) schools in the sample which had a government approved electric connection. In this regard, the teachers told that paying electricity bill on time is a huge problem for them as there are no specific provisions in the school budget nor are there any funds under Sarva Shiksha Abhiyan for electricity bills. The teachers told that, many a times, the teachers had to arrange the required funds on their own either by individual contribution or by collecting money from each student. Sometimes the village panchayats also provide the necessary monetary help to the school. Thus from the analysis it emerges that the VEDCs can certainly play a significant role on this aspect by networking with the local panchayats and the community people. But besides this the study recommends that the government must make some concrete and appropriate budgetary provisions so that the cost of electricity can be properly handled by the school.

Availability of Furniture

Availability of Furniture like chairs for teachers and benches for students is accorded very high importance under Sarva Shiksha Abhiyan. Otherwise also, the furniture for teachers and students is perceived to be of paramount importance by both the parents as well as the children. There is always a continuous demand for provisioning furniture in schools for a more conducive teaching learning environment (MHRD: 2008). In this context, the SSA Framework 2008 provides for separate funds for setting up suitable infrastructure including furniture for teachers and students.

Participation of community is mandatory in improving school facilities and to carry out civil works activities in a transparent manner (MHRD: 2008). Against this backdrop, it is attempted to know the status of availability of furniture in the sampled schools. The analysis revealed that as regards the availability of chairs to teachers, the situation was good as all the schools had chairs for the teachers. However it was not so with regard to the availability of tables to teachers because there was about one-fifth schools where there were no tables in the classrooms meant for the teacher's use like checking notebooks etc. So far as the availability of benches to students is concerned, the situation was unsatisfactory because in about three-fourth schools, there were no benches for the students. In these schools, the students either sat on mats provided by the school or they carried their own mats (fertilizer bags) along with them. The findings of the study are different than the study done by Juyal et al. (2007) who found that there were 65.22 per cent rural primary schools in Muktsar District and 41.67 per cent schools of Mansa District where there were no benches for students.

The present investigation reveals that though there has been an improvement over the years in the availability of furniture in the schools, however, the participation of VEDCs members in maintenance, upkeep and the purchase of furniture was observed to be minimal all along. It was observed during the field work that all the arrangements were being made by the head teacher or his colleagues alone while the VEDCs members just signed the purchase documents/vouchers without any follow up or a sense of ownership for the school amenities. It is, therefore, emphasized that the members of the VEDCs should work to ensure more cooperation towards the upkeep and the maintenance of the furniture in the schools. Overall the availability and the quality of furniture in the schools required a lot of improvement.

Availability of other Facilities

The analysis in this section reveals that 3.8 per cent schools in the sample did not had boundary walls. Nearly one-fifth (19.2%) schools in the sample did not have an open space worth playing for children. No school had manpower for maintaining the playgrounds nor were there any sport facilities like the balls, nets, rackets etc. In about 9.6 per cent schools there were no library/ book banks. First aids kits were not available in about 2 per cent schools. About 7.7 per cent schools did not even have a wall clock. This situation was inspite of the fact that the Sarva Shiksha Abhiyan earmarks special funds for all these amenities. SSA makes it mandatory for each district to provide the list of schools which requires major repairs like the school buildings, rooms or erecting four walls. The VEDCs are essentially required to make micro level plans indicating the school specific needs. Separate funds are provided to each school as per the demands made in the perspective plans. There is no dearth of funds for infrastructure and for procuring teaching learning materials, as such, under SSA. But even then, some schools remained deprived of the bare minimum facilities. This is indicative of the utter lack of will and involvement of the community people in the processes of school governance. Ironically some schools in the sample didn't even have first aid kits and wall clocks which, as such, required a very little investment. Such small things can easily be arranged through donations or even from philanthropists provided the community people and the school teachers exhibit a sense of belongingness to their school.

As regards other facilities, the analysis shows that the situation was reasonably good as far as the availability of things like black boards, chalks, dusters, almirahs/boxes and school bells was concerned.

The data depicts that the things like black boards, chalks, dusters, almirahs/boxes, school bells and mid day meals were although available in all the schools, but the quality and the maintenance of these facilities required immediate attention. For instance, with regard to the mid day meals, many teachers reported that the children hardly relish the food served while many parents lamented poor quality and irregularity in distribution of mid day meals to the children. Some of them even hinted at corrupt practices in the purchase of some food items. Similarly in many schools, the first aids kits, the books were not in usable condition. The almirahs and boxes for keeping school records were being very poorly maintained.

In this situation, the study underlines that apart from the availability, what is more important is the proper care and maintenance of the facilities by the appropriate stakeholders. The VEDCs, as such, have a significant role to play in the proper upkeep of facilities like the first aid kits, library, book banks, utensils as well as the mid day meals. Mere availability of such things is unlikely to fetch the desired results unless their quality is improved and secondly the people manning them show more commitment and accountability towards their optimal use. In today's era of competition, when the government schools are facing competition from the private schools, it is unreasonable to suggest that mere availability of the most the basic facilities like the black boards, almirahs and book banks etc. would improve the quality of education in rural schools.

The study, therefore, suggests that there is an urgency to further improve the school infrastructure so as to make it at par to that of the private schools and secondly the human factor in terms of teacher' characteristics should also be focused upon. The focus of attention needs to be both on the infrastructural facilities as well as the characteristics of teachers and the parents. Unless this paradigm shift take place, it is highly unlikely that the government schools would have any visible impact on the quality of education at the grassroots level. It is high time that the government and the community bring some radical changes in the school education apparatus itself. It is already clear that despite Punjab being at the top in school infrastructure (Education Development Index: 2011), a lot more is needed to improve the school education in terms of the quality, equity and the parity with the private schools. It is highly doubtful that mere availability of the most basic facilities in government schools would change the perception of the people or improve the quality of school education unless some radical changes in terms of human factors are brought about by the government urgently.

The Contribution of Village Education Development Committees

This section aims at analyzing the contribution of the Village Education Development Committee in terms of increase in school enrollment, reducing school dropout and improving school results. Besides this, the Section takes an overview of the activities undertaken by the VEDCs relating to improving infrastructure, fundraising and provisioning incentives to the students. In the light of the fifth objective of the study, the contribution of individual members and the issues relating to conduct of meetings have also been discussed at length in this section.

For exploring the change in enrollment, the change in the class-wise and gender-wise gross enrollment was calculated across three years period (2000-2003) before the formation of the VEDCs and for three years period (2003-2006) after the formation of the VEDCs. Likewise, the change in school drop-outs and school results was examined by calculating the difference between the absolute numbers of the students failed and dropped out in each year in each class over a period of three years (2000-2003) before the formation of the VEDCs and for three years period (2003-2006) after the formation of the VEDCs.

Increase in Enrollment

Village Education Development Committee is considered vital for providing a direct link between the community and the school in all education related issues. Enrollment being one such issues; increasing enrollment is one of the most important functions of this committee. The VEDC has to ensure that all the out-of-school children are enrolled in the village school and are provided all necessary help for a congenial learning environment. In this section, an attempt has been made to understand the extent to which VEDCs are helpful in increasing the enrollment of children in the schools. For this purpose, the information about class-wise enrollment has been collected from the school records for three years before the formation of VEDCs (2000-2003) and three years after the formation of VEDCs (2003-2006). Here it is worthwhile to mention again that the VEDCs in Punjab were officially launched in October 2002 by the then Congress Government. The first grant to the VEDCs was released only after the June 2003 Panchayat Election. This way the VEDCs started functioning in the year 2003.

In the present Section, the year-wise percentage increase/ decrease in the gross enrollment has been calculated to know the contribution of the VEDCs. Depending upon the percentage increase or decrease in gross enrollment, the trends has been analyzed for the period when the VEDCs were not formed and

Table 7.1: Class-wise and Year-wise Gross Enrollment in High Literacy Villages (N=26)

Before Formation of VEDCs

Year	*Gender*	*Class I*	*Class II*	*Class III*	*Class IV*	*Class V*	*Total*
2000-2001	Male	668	558	530	532	507	2795
	Female	503	491	432	451	421	2298
	Total	1171	1049	962	983	928	5093
2001-2002	Male	585	632	529	554	503	2803
	Female	524	518	448	402	424	2316
	Total	1109	1150	977	956	927	5119
Change*	Male	-12.42	+13.26	-0.18	+4.13	-0.78	+0.28
	Female	+4.17	+5.49	+3.70	-10.86	+0.71	+0.78
	Total	-5.29	+9.62	+1.55	-2.74	-0.10	+0.51
2002-2003	Male	598	608	607	531	529	2873
	Female	492	503	487	453	419	2354
	Total	1090	1111	1094	984	948	5227
Change*	Male	+2.23	-3.79	+14.74	-4.15	+5.16	+2.49
	Female	-6.10	-2.89	+8.70	+12.68	-1.17	+1.64
	Total	-1.71	-3.39	+11.97	+2.92	+2.26	+2.10

After Formation of VEDCs

Year	*Gender*	*Class I*	*Class II*	*Class III*	*Class IV*	*Class V*	*Total*
2003-2004	Male	573	593	582	589	531	2868
	Female	490	497	509	483	432	2411
	Total	1063	1090	1091	1072	963	5279
2004-2005	Male	621	572	608	589	561	2951
	Female	530	484	464	477	492	2447
	Total	1151	1056	1072	1066	1053	5398
	Male	+8.37	-3.54	+4.46	0	+5.64	+2.89
Change*	Female	+8.16	-2.61	-8.84	-1.24	+13.88	+1.49
	Total	+8.27	-3.11	-1.74	-0.55	+9.34	+2.25
2005-2006	Male	605	606	630	637	595	3073
	Female	550	581	609	621	583	2944
	Total	1155	1187	1239	1258	1178	6017
Change*	Male	-2.57	+5.94	+3.61	+8.14	+6.06	+4.13
	Female	+3.77	+20.04	+31.25	+30.18	+18.49	+20.31
	Total	+0.34	+12.40	+15.57	+18.01	+11.87	+11.46

* Minus and Plus signs respectively denote the percentage Decrease and Increase with respect to the previous year

the period when they were put in place. The discussions have been done separately for the high literacy villages and the low literacy villages and are presented in Table 7.1. The inferences have been drawn under the assumption that the increase in enrollment, if any, had happened due to the existence of VEDCs, regardless of other facilitating or impeding factors thereupon.

High Literacy Villages

It is evident from the data that before the formation of the VEDCs, the gross enrollment in the sampled schools in the high literacy regions, increased by 0.51 per cent from year 2000-01 to year 2001-02 and from 2001-02 to 2002-03 the gross enrollment increased by 2.10 per cent. After the formation of VEDCs, the enrollment increased by 2.25 per cent from 2003-04 to 2004-05 and by 11.46 per cent from 2004-05 to 2005-06. This shows that the rate of increase in the gross enrollment was higher after the formation of the VEDCs in the high literacy villages.

Thus from the analysis it can be suggested that since the percentage increase in the gross enrollment in the high literacy villages was higher after the formation of VEDCs in comparison to the year wise percentage increase witnessed before the formation of the VEDCs, the Village Education Development Committees can be said to have contributed positively towards this trend regardless of other factors which might have had their own impact.

As regards the gender wise analysis, the data reveals that the gross enrollment of the girls before the formation of VEDCs has increased by 0.78 per cent from 2000-01 to 2001-02 period and there was an increase of 1.64 per cent in the next year i.e. from 2001-02 to 2002-03. After the formation of VEDCs, the gross enrollment across girls has increased by bigger margins in comparison to the increase happening before the formation of the VEDCs. For example, the girls' gross enrollment increased by 1.49 per cent during 2003-04 and 2004-05 whereas the increase was 20.31 per cent during 2004-05 and 2005-06 period. This increase was much less during 2000-01 to 2001-02 and 2001-02 to 2002-03 respectively. Thus from this trend, it can be suggested that the VEDCs must have had a positive contribution towards increasing girls' gross enrollment in the high literacy regions.

As regards the gross enrollment of boys, there was a consistent increase in the enrollment before as well as after the formation of VEDCs in the high literacy regions. Just has in case of girls, the percentage increase was higher after the formation of VEDCs

Table 7.2: Class-wise and Year-wise Gross Enrollment in Low Literacy Villages (N=26)

Before Formation of VEDCs

Year	Gender	Class I	Class II	Class III	Class IV	Class V	Total
2000-2001	Male	452	481	525	505	529	2492
	Female	428	402	416	447	446	2139
	Total	880	883	941	952	975	4631
2001-2002	Male	479	456	439	515	453	2342
	Female	347	415	435	440	419	2056
	Total	826	871	874	955	872	4398
Change*	Male	+5.97	-5.19	-16.38	+1.98	-14.36	-6.01
	Female	-18.92	+3.23	+4.56	-1.56	-6.05	-3.88
	Total	-6.13	-1.35	-7.12	+0.31	-10.56	-5.03
2002-2003	Male	559	496	427	509	474	2465
	Female	386	406	405	450	442	2089
	Total	945	902	832	959	916	4554
Change*	Male	+16.70	+8.77	-2.73	-1.16	+4.63	+5.25
	Female	+11.23	-2.16	-6.89	+2.27	+5.48	+1.60
	Total	+14.40	+3.55	-4.80	+0.41	+5.04	+3.54

After Formation of VEDCs

Year	Gender	Class I	Class II	Class III	Class IV	Class V	Total
2003-2004	Male	497	604	503	480	453	2537
	Female	398	417	404	452	412	2083
	Total	895	1021	907	935	865	4620
	Male	544	483	556	450	464	2497
2004-2005	Female	450	383	412	357	398	2000
	Total	994	866	968	807	862	4497
	Male	+9.45	-20.03	+10.53	-6.83	+2.42	-1.57
Change*	Female	+13.06	-8.15	+1.98	-21.01	-3.39	-3.98
	Total	+11.06	-15.18	+6.72	-13.68	-0.34	-2.72
	Male	536	490	552	436	432	2446
2005-2006	Female	439	382	401	319	369	1910
	Total	975	872	953	755	801	4356
Change*	Male	-1.47	+1.44	-0.71	-3.11	-6.89	-2.04
	Female	-2.45	-0.27	-2.66	-10.64	-7.28	-4.5
	Total	-1.91	+0.69	-1.54	-6.44	-7.07	-3.13

* Minus and Plus signs respectively denote the percentage Decrease and Increase with respect to the previous year

which is suggestive of the fact that, withstanding all facilitating and impeding factors, the VEDCs must have had a positive contribution towards increasing the gross enrollment of boys in the area of the present study.

Overall, it can be suggested from the data that in high literacy villages, the VEDCs contributed positively towards increasing the enrollment of students in the sampled schools.

Low Literacy Villages

The analysis revealed that the trends in the low literacy villages were not uniform with regard to percentage change in the gross enrollment of students in the sampled schools. The figures depict that before the formation of VEDCs, there was a decrease of 5.03 per cent from the year 2000-01 to 2001-02 whereas in the following year (from 2001-02 to 2002-03), the enrollment increased by 3.54 per cent. After the formation of the VEDCs, the enrollment dropped by 2.72 per cent during the first year (2003-04 to 2004-05) and by 3.13 per cent in the following year (2004-05 to 2005-06). Thus it is obvious from the findings that the formation of VEDCs did not make any significant contribution with regard to the increase in enrollment of students in the low literacy villages.

The trends across the gender of students followed the similar pattern. It is evident that before the formation of VEDCs, the enrollment of girls witnessed a drop of 3.88 per cent during 2000-01 and 2001-02 period whereas there was an increase of 1.60 per cent in the following year (2001-02 to 2002-03). After the VEDCs were formed, the enrollment of girls dropped by 3.98 per cent in the first year of formation (2003-04 to 2004-05) and by 4.5 per cent during the second year of formation (2004-05 to 2005-06). Now it is clear that the after the formation of VEDCs, the enrollment dropped instead of escalating. Same trends were witnessed in case of boys. This means that the formation of VEDCs did not play any positive role towards increasing the enrollment of students in the schools situated in low literacy villages. Overall, the analysis suggests that in the low literacy villages, the contribution of the VEDCs in increasing the enrollment of students was not visible as the gross enrollment of students witnessed a consistent drop even after the formation of VEDCs.

Reduction in School Drop-Out Rate and Improving School Results

The reduction in school dropout has been studied by analyzing the difference between the absolute numbers of students dropped out each year in each class in the sampled schools over a period of three years (2000-03) before the formation of the VEDCs and three years after the formation of the VEDCs (2003-06). Similarly the improvement in school results have been studied by analyzing the difference in number of students failed each year in each class for three years (2000-03) before the formation of VEDCs and three years after the formation of the VEDCs (2003-06). The data has been analyzed separately for the high and low literacy villages.

Improvement in School Results

For academic convenience, the decrease in the number of failures (students who failed) was considered to be one of the parameters for the improvement in the school results. The trends in the per cent change (increase/decrease) were examined to suggest whether or not the VEDCs played any role towards improving the results of the schools in the sample ignoring all other factors acting simultaneously towards improving or not improving the school results.

High Literacy Villages

The data depicts that the number of the students who failed in the annual examinations across all the classes in all the schools in the sample were 137 in the year 2000-01 whereas this number came down to 79 students in the following year 2001-02. This way, there was a 42.33 per cent decline in the number of failures during this period. Further, during the year 2002-03, the total number of students who could not pass the examinations increased to 128 students showing a huge increase of 62.02 per cent in comparison to the previous year 2001-02. This analysis suggests that before the formation of VEDCs, the results have shown an improvement during 2000-01 and 2001-02 whereas in the following year, the results were very poor as the number of failures has increased to a great extent. After the formation of VEDCs, there was no sign of improvement in the school results.

The data reveals that the number of failures increased from 103 in year 2003-04 to 128 students in year 2004-05 indicating an increase of 24.27 per cent. Next year (2005-06) the number of failures decreased to 113 students showing a decrease of 11.7 per cent in the number of failures and thus indicting an improvement in the school results. From the analysis, it is evident that the trends followed a zigzag path as in the first year (2003-04) of formation of VEDCs; the result did not show any improvement while in the subsequent year (2005-06) the results showed improvement. Same zigzag path was followed before the formation of VEDCs as in the first year (2000-01 to 2001-02), the results improved while in the next year (2001-02 to 2002-03), the trend was opposite. So it can be suggested that the VEDCs had not played any role in improving the school results in the high literacy villages.

Low Literacy Villages

The data revealed that over a period of three years before the formation of VEDCs, the number of failures increased each year. In the first year (2000-01), the number of failures was 155 while in the subsequent year (2001-02), the number increased to 157 students indicating an increase of 1.29 per cent. Similarly the number of students who failed to pass the annual examination during the year 2002-03 increased to 166 students showing a further increase of 5.73 per cent. This way it is evident that the school results did not show any improvement during 2000-01 and 2002-03. After the formation of VEDCs, the analysis revealed an opposite trend as there was a dramatic decrease in the number of failures in the sampled schools. It can be seen from the data that during 2003-04 and 2004-05, there was a huge drop of 56.7 per cent in the number of failures and similarly a drop of 22.89 per cent was witnessed during 2004-05 and 2005-06. As the decrease in the failures has been considered as one of the parameters indicating improved school results, it can be suggested that the school results have improved after the formation of VEDCs in the low literacy regions. Thus it is concluded that withstanding other factors, the VEDCs played a positive role towards reducing the number of failures thus improving the school results.

Table 7.3: Class wise and year wise School Result and Reduction in Drop-out Rate in High Literacy Villages (N=26)

Before Formation of VEDCs

Year	Gender	Class I		Class II		Class III		Class IV		Class V		Total	
		Failed	Drop-outs	Failed	Drop-outs	Failed	Drop-outs	Failed	Drop-outs	Failed	Drop-outs	Failed	Drop-outs
2000-2001	Male	24	16	24	05	06	02	22	03	04	01	80	27
	Female	12	5	12	2	11	1	12	5	10	2	57	15
	Total	36	21	36	7	17	3	34	8	14	3	137	42
2001-2002	Male	4	9	10	0	10	3	11	0	2	3	37	15
	Female	13	13	2	3	8	0	13	1	6	3	42	20
	Total	17	22	12	3	18	3	24	1	8	6	79	35
Change*	Male	-83.3	-43.7	-58.3	-100	+66.6	+50	-50	-100	-50	+200	-53.7	-44.4
	Female	+8.3	+80	-83.3	+50	-27.2	-100	+8.3	-80	-40	+50	-26.3	+33.3
	Total	-52.7	-38.0	-66.6	-57.14	+5.8	00	-29.4	-87.5	-42.8	+100	-42.3	-16.6
2002-2003	Male	9	9	22	2	17	1	8	0	12	0	68	12
	Female	11	6	20	3	9	0	11	1	9	1	60	11
	Total	20	15	42	5	26	1	19	1	21	1	128	23
Change*	Male	+125	0	+120	+200	+70	-33.3	-27.2	0	+500	-100	+83.7	-20
	Female	-15.3	-53.8	+900	0	+12.5	0	-15.3	0	+50	-66.6	+42.8	-45
	Total	+17.6	-31.8	+250	+66.67	+44.4	-33.3	-20.8	0	+162.5	-83.3	+62.0	-34.2

After Formation of VEDCs

Year	Gender	Class I		Class II		Class III		Class IV		Class V		Total	
		Failed	Drop outs	Failed	Drop outs	Failed	Drop outs	Failed	Drop outs	Failed	Drop outs	Failed	Drop outs
2003-2004	Male	5	13	13	3	11	0	15	2	5	2	49	20
	Female	7	3	15	0	18	4	7	2	7	2	54	11
	Total	12	16	28	3	29	4	22	4	12	4	103	31
2004-2005	Male	1	13	14	8	20	8	21	11	19	8	75	48
	Female	1	18	11	13	6	1	16	8	19	4	53	44
	Total	2	31	25	21	26	9	37	19	38	12	128	92
Change*	Male	-80	0	+7.6	+166.6	+81.8	+800	+40	+450	+280	+300	+53.0	+140
	Female	-85.7	+500	-26.6	+1300	-66.6	-75	+128.5	+300	+171.4	+100	-1.8	+300
	Total	-83.3	+93.7	-10.7	+600	-10.3	+125	+68.1	+375	+216.6	+200	+24.2	+196.7
2005-2006	Male	8	5	20	2	15	1	11	4	13	2	67	14
	Female	9	8	13	5	11	0	7	2	6	3	46	18
	Total	17	13	33	7	26	1	18	6	19	5	113	32
Change*	Male	+700	-61.5	+42.8	-75	-25	-87.5	-47.6	-63.6	-31.5	-75	-10.6	-70.8
	Female	+800	-55.5	+18.1	-61.5	+83.8	-100	-56.2	-75	-68.4	-25	-13.2	-59.0
	Total	+750	-58.0	+32	-66.6	0	-88.8	-51.3	-68.4	-50	-58.3	-11.7	-65.2

* Minus and Plus signs respectively denote the percentage Decrease and Increase with respect to the previous year

Reduction in School Drop outs

The data on drop outs was collected from the school records. As mentioned earlier the reduction in school dropout has been studied by analyzing the difference between the absolute numbers of students dropped out each year in each class in the sampled schools over a period of three years (2000-03) before the formation of VEDCs and three years after the formation of the VEDCs (2003-06).The analysis have been done separately for the higher literacy and the low literacy regions.

High Literacy Villages

It is clear from the data that in the year 2000-01, the number of drop-outs in all the sampled schools was 42 while in the year 2001-02, the number reduced to 35 showing a drop of 16.67 per cent. Likewise, the drop out was further reduced to 23 students in the following year 2002-03 indicating a decline of 34.28 per cent. This means that there was a reduction in the dropout rate even without the VEDCs being in place. After the formation of the VEDCs, the drop out increased from 31 students in year 2003-04 to 92 students in the year 2004-05 showing a whopping increase of 196.7 per cent. In the subsequent year 2005-06, the number of dropout witnessed a decrease of 65.21 per cent. This shows that the dropout rate increased during the first year of formation o VEDCs while it reduced in the second year showing a zigzag pattern in the trends. This suggests that the VEDCs did not play a positive role as far as reduction of dropout rate in high literacy regions is concerned.

Low Literacy Villages

In the low literacy villages, before formation of VEDCs, the dropout rate was increased by 57.14 per cent from 2000-01 to 2001-02 whereas for the subsequent year i.e. from 2001-02 to 2002-03, the dropout rate decreased by 32.72 per cent. Thus before the formation of the VEDCs, the number of drop outs increased during the first year while the number of drop outs decreased during the second year. After the formation of VEDCs, no change was observed in the trends as during the year 2003-04 and 2004-05, the dropout

Table 7.4: Class wise and year wise School Result and Reduction in Drop-out Rate in Low Literacy Villages (N=26)

Before Formation of VEDCs

Year	Gender	Class I		Class II		Class III		Class IV		Class V		Total	
		Failed	Drop outs	Failed	Drop outs	Failed	Drop outs	Failed	Drop outs	Failed	Drop outs	Failed	Drop outs
2000-2001	Male	23	13	10	2	12	0	21	2	10	2	76	19
	Female	24	12	11	3	13	0	15	1	16	0	79	16
	Total	47	25	21	5	25	0	36	3	26	2	155	35
2001-2002	Male	24	17	19	1	24	2	14	2	6	2	87	24
	Female	9	10	20	4	15	7	14	10	12	0	70	31
	Total	33	27	39	5	39	9	28	12	18	2	157	55
Change*	Male	+4.3	+30.7	+90	-50	+100	+200	-33.3	0	-40	0	+14.4	+26.3
	Female	-62.5	-16.6	+81.8	+33.3	+15.3	+700	-6.6	+900	-25	0	-11.3	+93.7
	Total	-29.7	+8.0	+85.7	0	+56.0	+900	-22.2	+300	-30.7	0	+1.2	+57.1
2002-2003	Male	16	5	13	4	20	0	21	2	7	0	77	11
	Female	21	5	19	3	16	4	26	12	7	2	89	26
	Total	37	10	32	7	36	4	47	14	14	2	166	37
Change*	Male	-33.3	-70.5	-31.5	+300	-16.6	-100	+50	0	+1.6	-100	-11.4	-54.1
	Female	+12.1	-50	-5.0	-25	-6.7	-42.8	+85.7	+20	-41.6	+200	+27.1	-16.1
	Total	+133.3	-62.9	-17.9	+40	-7.6	-55.5	+67.8	+16.6	-22.2	0	+5.7	-32.7

After Formation of VEDCs

Year	Gender	Class I		Class II		Class III		Class IV		Class V		Total	
		Failed	Drop outs	Failed	Drop outs	Failed	Drop outs	Failed	Drop outs	Failed	Drop outs	Failed	Drop outs
2003-2004	Male	17	17	39	8	23	7	22	5	10	0	111	37
	Female	9	7	21	2	25	10	19	2	7	0	81	21
	Total	26	24	60	10	48	17	41	7	17	0	192	58
2004-2005	Male	4	15	8	11	9	16	17	10	13	17	51	69
	Female	1	17	9	10	8	16	7	4	7	3	32	50
	Total	5	32	17	21	17	32	24	14	20	20	83	119
Change*	Male	-76.4	-11.7	-79.4	+37.5	-60.8	+128	-22.7	+100	+30	+1700	-54.0	+86.4
	Female	-88.8	+142.8	-57.1	+400	-68	+60	-63.1	+100	0	+300	-60.4	+138.0
	Total	-80.7	+33.3	-71.6	+110	-64.5	+88.2	-41.4	+100	+17.6	+2000	-56.7	+105.1
2005-2006	Male	3	12	7	12	7	12	12	0	10	11	39	47
	Female	2	15	8	9	10	11	3	1	2	0	25	36
	Total	5	27	15	21	17	23	15	1	12	11	64	83
Change*	Male	-25	-20	-12.5	+9.0	-22.2	-25	-29.4	-100	-23.0	-35.2	-23.5	-31.8
	Female	+100	-11.7	-11.1	-10	+25	-31.2	-57.1	-75	-71.4	-300	-28.0	-28
	Total	0	-15.6	-11.7	0	0	-28.1	-37.5	-92.8	-40	-45	-22.8	-30.2

* Minus and Plus signs respectively denote the percentage Decrease and Increase with respect to the previous year.

rate increased significantly by 105.17 per cent while the dropout rate reduced by 35.25 per cent during the subsequent period extending from 2004-05 to 2005-06.

The data shows that during the first year of the formation of the VEDCs, the rate of drop out increased significantly whereas during the second year, the rate of drop out decreased quite a bit indicating an inconsistent trend which suggested that the VEDCs did not play any significant role towards reduction of school dropout in the low literacy villages. Thus from the analysis, it can be suggested that the VEDCs did not play any significant role in reducing the school dropout rate in the sampled schools situated in the low literacy villages of Muktsar and Mansa districts. Overall, the contribution of VEDCs in reducing dropout was insignificant.

Contribution of VEDCs Members in Individual Capacity

This section is devoted to explore the contribution of individual members in terms of any visit or interaction with any of the stakeholders with a view to improve the teaching learning environment in the school. The observation during the course of field work revealed that there were significantly very few members of the VEDCs who demonstrated a keen interest in the school affairs. From the data it is evident that only about one-fifth (20.0%) members had discussed the problems of the school with the appropriate officials or the parents and that too just once or twice in their full tenure as VEDC member. Similarly a little more than one-fifth (22.4%) members had paid one or two visits to the school with an aim of monitoring the school environment. The data further revealed that the member-teacher interaction on issues relating to school improvement was minimal. Only about 35.8 per cent members gave an affirmative reply to the question of member-teacher interaction.

The observation revealed that the members who agreed to have interacted with the teachers talked to them only once or twice only during their tenure. As regards the contribution of members towards arranging funds/donations for the school, 44.0 per cent members told that they have collected money for organizing sports activities in the school. From further break-up of the data, it was found that 90.4 per cent head teachers agreed to have interacted with teachers on ways and means of improving the school environment while 67.3 per cent of the head teachers have discussed the problems of the school with appropriate authorities of the government from time to time.

In general, the findings suggest that the contribution of individual members of the VEDCs with regard to school improvement has not been very encouraging except for the head teachers. Thus there lies a need to initiate some programme aimed at boosting the morale of the VEDCs members such that they develop a feeling of belongingness towards their school as mandated under Sarva Shiksha Abhiyan.

Conduct of Meetings

This section gives an elaborate account of issues relating to the conduct of VEDCs meetings with reference to number of meetings, attendance of members and the issues discussed in the meetings. The guidelines state that the monthly meeting of VEDC is compulsory. The VEDC is required to hold at least one meeting between 2nd and 7th day every month. If need arises more than one meeting can also be held. The record of the resolutions passed in these meetings will essentially be maintained. This meeting will be held in the school as per pre-decided date and time. The notice of the meeting shall be issued by the member secretary. The VEDC meeting shall be held within the school only. In case, any member of the committee remains absent in three consecutive meetings, his membership shall be cancelled and a new member shall be nominated in his place. The position of any VEDC member shall not remain vacant for more than three months in any case. The VEDC chairman or any other member of the VEDC shall not, in any case, ask to bring any record pertaining to school or meeting outside the school premises. For signing any document, the VEDC chairman shall himself come to the school. It is the sole responsibility of the member secretary to maintain the accounts and get the work completed. The present study found that the meetings of the VEDCs are not held in accordance with the guidelines laid down by the Sarva Shiksha Abhiyan Authority Punjab and most of the aforementioned norms regarding conduct of meetings of these bodies are not followed in letter and spirit.

The forthcoming section would make the point clearer with empirical evidences. The discussion is centred around three major issues with regard to the conduct of meetings namely the number of meetings held in one year, the attendance of members in the meetings and the issues discussed in the VEDC meetings.

Number of VEDC Meetings

As regards the minimum number of VEDC meetings supposed to be held in one year, about 79.3 per cent respondents knew that at least one meeting of VEDC is compulsory in a month. These respondents told that a meeting has to be convened every month except during the summer vacations, however, in practice, the VEDCs meeting is called only when any grant is received by the school. It may not necessarily be between the 2nd and 7th of every month as mandated in the guidelines. To the second query as to how many meetings were held in 2007-08 (the data was collected during 2008-2009), nearly three-fifth (59.1%) respondents replied that eleven meetings were held while 27.7 per cent told that ten meetings were held that year.

In the course of field work, it was found that the meetings of the VEDCs are not at all a monthly feature. In fact, no formal meetings of the VEDCs are held. Instead whenever a grant is received, the head teacher/secretary after recording the minutes on his own, sends the register to the residences of the VEDCs members for signatures. As such the meetings of the VEDCs are held on papers only. The record of the minutes available with the secretary revealed that most of the VEDC meetings are held for sorting out the issues relating to civil works and utilization of grants received from time to time.

Attendance in VEDC Meetings

As pointed out earlier, the meetings of the VEDCs are held only on papers. The issues of agenda of the VEDCs meeting are mainly relating to the utilization of grants or some resolutions regarding construction or civil works in the schools. The Secretary records the minutes of the meetings on a particular issue and get the signatures of members in circulation. The secretaries/head teachers revealed that despite the persistent requests, the VEDC members don't come to the school for meetings. It is the primary reason why the VEDC meetings are to be held in circulation. Surprisingly, a huge majority (89.5%) of the VEDC members themselves were candid enough to have agreed that the members don't give any importance to the VEDC meetings. For most members the VEDCs are not a priority issue as they viewed the meetings of VEDCs as a formality. The members told that as the VEDCs meetings don't serve any purpose; attending or not attending them does not make any difference. The present results are in some way substantiated by the findings of Tyagi (1999) who revealed that in Bihar about half of the VEC members were not attending the meetings regularly nor were they participating in any school related activities. Nayak (2002) also found that majority of the members in Orissa didn't attend the meetings. However, Sujatha and Rao (2000) found that in Andhra Pradesh, the situation was better as about 80 per cent heads of the households, even those who were not VEC members, attended the VEC meetings.

From the analysis, it can be concluded that the situation of members attending the VEDC meetings in Punjab was the worst. It is because there is no attendance of the VEDCs members in the meetings nor the meetings of VEDCs in the area of the study are held regularly and in a formal manner.

General lack of interest among the teachers as well as the VEDC members towards VEDCs was quite evident and it was one of the primary reasons of the dismal state of affairs of the VEDCs as far as the attendance of the members in the meetings is concerned. Therefore it can be suggested that there is a need to reorient the VEDC members as well as the teachers such that they begin to value the importance of VEDCs and their meetings.

Issues Discussed in the Meetings

The quality of school education, inter alia, revolves around teachers' characteristics, infrastructure, support services, curriculum, teaching learning material, classroom processes and so on. As per the SSA mandate, the VEDCs are expected to act as the custodian of all the issues that determines the educational outcomes at the village level. So in order to understand the contribution of VEDCs, it was thought essential to identify the issues that are usually recorded or never recorded in minutes of the meetings of the VEDCs. For this purpose, the views of the members of the VEDCs were sought and analyzed on a three point scale i.e. the issues that forms the agenda items in all the meetings, in some meetings and the issues that are never taken up. Here it may be pointed out once again that the meetings of these bodies are usually held in circulation. A perusal of the data revealed that there are two major issues that always find a place in the minutes of the VEDC meetings. These relate to making provisions for infrastructural facilities like construction of rooms, repair of buildings, purchase of furniture and other such civil or maintenance jobs. Second issue related to the utilization of grants. It was, in fact, known during the investigation that the VEDC meetings are called only when there is some issue relating to infrastructure or utilization of grants else no need is felt for a meeting. From the data, it is evident that about 88.8 per cent VEDC members expressed that issues relating to infrastructure are the primary issues of all meetings, followed by the issues regarding utilization of grants as mentioned by 88.3 per cent respondents. Another issue that finds mention in the minutes of some of the meetings related to the enrollment of out-of-school children in the village (84.7%). The issues that are never mentioned in the VEDCs meetings were regarding reducing school dropout (78.3%) and improving the school results (84.2%), monitoring the teachers (88.6%) and addressing problems of the children (76.2%).

It is clear from the analysis that the major focus of VEDCs remain on the issues that are unavoidably essential under the prescribed rules like the proper of utilization of grants and civil works. The findings corroborate the arguments of Mor (2008) who reiterates that VEDCs in Punjab discuss only those issues which involve money like the construction of building and toilets. The quality issues like teaching learning processes in the classroom don't find a place in interaction between the stakeholders.

It may be mentioned here that in matters involving money, an omission, even if inadvertent, would straightway lead to some serious disciplinary action which is why the Secretary is extra careful in completing all paper work in this regard like maintaining the proceedings of meetings and getting signatures from all the people as per official requirements. The quality issues like teaching learning material, classroom processes and learning achievements etc. are not considered of much worth for the meetings as avoidance of these issues don't entail any serious punishment. The recording or not recording of such issues in the minutes, hardly, has any serious disciplinary implications. In the light of the above, the major focus of the VEDCs meetings remain only on such issues avoidance of which leads to punishment or an explanation by the appropriate officials of the Education Department of the State Government.

Activities of the VEDCs

Sarva Shiksha Abhiyan is an effort to universalize elementary education by community ownership of school system. To operationalize this component, the VEDCs has to play a significant role in micro planning, preparing school development plans besides provisioning for other appropriate teaching aids and resources. Against this background, a strong need was felt to identify the activities of the VEDCs that lead to school ownership of the school system as envisioned in the SSA Framework. For the sake of clarity and academic convenience, the activities have been studied under four broad categories namely:

a) Activities for improving school infrastructure
b) Activities for fund raising
c) Activities for provisioning incentives for students
d) General/Miscellaneous activities

The data presented and analyzed in this section indicates the information for the year 2007-08. It is because the data for the present study was collected in year 2008 and 2009 and only of those VEDCs that were formed between June 2003 panchayat elections and May 2008 panchayat elections.

Activities undertaken to Improve Infrastructure

A perusal of the data makes it clear that a huge majority of the VEDCs members (91.5%) replied in affirmative to the query as to whether the VEDC that they represent had carried out any activity for improving the school infrastructure. Out of these respondents, 81.1 per cent informed that the major activities undertaken by the VEDC were about repairing and constructing the classrooms followed by repairing and constructing the toilets and ramps (70.4%). Nearly one-third (28.19%) respondents (N=376) told that the VEDC repaired/constructed boundary wall of the school whereas a little more than one-tenth (11.1%) of these respondents informed that the Committee purchased furniture for teachers and students. It is worth mentioning here that the Sarva Shiksha Abhiyan assigns greatest importance to the civil and maintenance activities and provides sufficient funds for construction of classrooms, school building and other basic facilities like toilets, ramps and furniture. These facilities have been conceived as necessary pre-requisites for quality implementation of the Programme. The participation of community in the form of VEDCs in all civil works is mandatory in order to ensure a sense of ownership for the school. It is obligatory for the VEDCs to utilize the funds properly and keep ready all the records in terms of all payments, receipts and the vouchers for any inspection. The findings of the present study revealed that the major focus of the VEDCs in the sample has been on repairs and construction activities. The accounts are properly maintained and jointly operated by the Secretary and the Chairman. There was no marked difference across the high and low literacy villages on this aspect.

Activities for Fundraising

The allocation of resources under Sarva Shiksha Abhiyan is dependent on the Perspective Plans and Annual Plans prepared by each district according to the existing requirements. The Perspective Plan is a dynamic document worked out on the basis of feedback and the requirements of the school in terms of both infrastructure and teaching learning materials. The broad financial norms are set out as per this Plan and the resources are reimbursed as per the broad indicators available for a district in the Plan. The Perspective Plans are necessarily to be prepared with the involvement of the VEDCs. It is highly unlikely that the funds are not allocated as per the estimates shown in the Perspective Plan.

Against this scenario, an attempt has been made in this Section to explore whether the VEDCs undertake any activity for raising more funds for further supplementing the SSA funds meant for the general welfare of the village school and the school going children. As expected, it was found that a majority of the VEDCs don't actually carry out any activity for supplementing the government funds. The statistics revealed that 87.3 per cent VEDCs members replied in the negative when asked if their VEDC had undertaken any fundraising activity. About 12.7 per cent members informed that the VEDC they represent had collected donations for organizing some sports events. Of them, some said to have asked the Sarpanch to give some money from the panchayat grants for the school. Some NRIs were also requested for donations. In general, the fundraising activities by the VEDCs are negligible and there were hardly any variations on this issue across the low and high literacy villages.

Activities towards providing Incentives to Students

Reaching out to girls and the children from the disadvantaged sections of the society is central to the efforts to universalize elementary education under Sarva Shiksha Abhiyan. The Programme calls for involving participatory processes to bring the out-of-school children to the school. The targeted provisions for the girls and SC/ST children include free text books/notebooks, special mainstreaming efforts like the remedial/coaching classes, bridge courses, incentives like the uniforms and scholarships etc. These provisions are context-specific and require interventions designed to suit the specific community needs (MHRD SSA Framework: 2008).

Against the foregoing scenario, the present section makes an attempt to understand the contribution of VEDCs in managing these activities/schemes in the sampled schools. In the course of field work, it was found that the major incentives being implemented with the help of the VEDCs include free text books/notebooks, exposure visits, remedial/coaching classes, cash prizes for toppers and the judo karate workshops. The data on this aspect revealed that as per 82.5 per cent VEDC members, the VEDCs organized exposure visits for the school children whereas 79.6 per cent respondents told that free text books/notebooks schemes being monitored by these committees. As per 77.6 per cent respondents, the VEDCS were involved in giving cash prizes to the first three toppers of each class in every school. Other activities where the VEDCs participated related to vocational courses for girls like the course on computer literacy, embroidery and soft skills. VEDCs also extended help in organizing judo karate workshops as told by 64.5 per cent members. From the field work, it is known that the VEDCs participate only in those activities which are sponsored either by the State or the Central Government. There was no scheme/incentive known to have been launched by the VEDCs themselves i.e. by generating their own funds. All the schemes/incentives were being sponsored either by the State Government or the Sarva Shiksha Abhiyan Authority. As regards the help from the members of the VEDCs provided to the school teachers towards proper management of the incentives for students, more than three-fifth respondents agreed that the members had reasonable involvement in the successful implementation of these incentives. On this aspect there was a discernible difference between the high and low literacy villages as the proportion of the responses was much lower (56.6%) in low literacy regions as compared to the high literacy villages (69.2%).

General/Miscellaneous Activities

The VEDCs under Sarva Shiksha Abhiyan have been formed to enable the community members to participate in the management, improvement, administration and supervision of the elementary schools in their community. The VEDCs are expected to contribute to the access related issues in terms of getting out-of-school children into the main-fold and ensure that they stay there. Besides this, these bodies are mandated to address the quality dimensions by ensuring, among other things, the teachers' attendance and quality classroom processes. These bodies have to display a significant role in equity issues by helping children with special needs to integrate with the normal children. In nutshell, the VEDCs have to meet the goals of quality oriented educational outputs by enhancing enrollment, retention and the learning achievements of the school going children, thereby, improving the overall academic environment at the village level (MHRD-SSA Framework:2008). Against this scenario, the present section deals with the activities undertaken by the VEDCs to encourage good practices and suitable conditions for improving the school

Table 7.5: General/Miscellaneous Activities

Sl. No.	*Activities*	*Distribution of Respondents*		*Total*
		Yes	*No*	
Did the VEDC carried out some activities for improving the Academic Environment at the Village Level?		60 (14.6)	351 (85.4)	411 (100)
Yes Response (N=60)		High Literacy	Low Literacy	Total
1	Held door to door meetings/discussions with the parents	9 (15)	4 (6.67)	13 (21.6)
2	Speaking to local activists about problems of school	7 (11.6)	3 (5)	10 16.6)
3	Organized cultural programmes/games	18 (30)	20 (33.3)	38 63.3)
4	Organized sensitisation lectures for parents of children	8 (13.3)	5 (8.3)	13 21.6)
5	Made announcements from time to time from the Gurudwara	18 (30)	22 (36.6)	40 66.6)
6	Put up activity boards at prominent places	21 (35)	19 (31.6)	40 66.6)

Multiple Response Table
Source: Sample Survey
Figures in parentheses denote percentages

environment at the community level. The analysis made it that a huge majority of respondents (85.4%) were of the view that the VEDCs did not undertake any activity other than those mandated under government norms. However, 14.6 per cent respondents held an opposite view and told that the VEDCs they represented had undertaken one or the other activities for increasing enrollment and school results and reducing dropout. The major activities reported by these respondents included putting up of boards at various places within the village displaying the details of civil works and utilization of grants, making announcements from the gurudwaras from time to time regarding various school related issues. Besides this, the VEDCs also organized cultural programme and sports activities in some schools. Other activities as reported by the VEDCs members were holding door to door meetings, organizing lectures and speaking to local activists/community leaders about the problems at the school.

The present claims can be reinforced by the findings of Kumar et al. (1999) who found that the members of VECs in Gujarat usually participated in the celebrations of national days, sports days and result declaration day. In some cases PTA also sponsored some activities like the school magazine and sports etc. From the analysis it can be suggested that the contribution of VEDCs towards school related activities other than those mandated under SSA guidelines is very poor. This aspect is indicative of the lack of initiative and motivation among the VEDCs members towards school improvement. Therefore it is very urgent to design some mechanisms for activating the members for a more proactive involvement in initiating new activities for quality school education. The VEDCs members need to be sensitized to value the importance of community participation in school activities for positive educational outcomes.

The Problems of VEDCs and Suggestions

This section focuses on the problems of the VEDCs as stated by the members of the VEDCs. Apart from that the section also provides the suggestions to improve the functioning of these bodies. Since the establishment of these bodies in October 2002, the VEDCs, on the whole, have largely failed to make a mark on the education apparatus of the State. It is conveniently accepted that the VEDCs have not been able to carve a niche for themselves at the village level due to many problems of the perceptional, functional and administrative nature. Some of such problems (as perceived by the members of VEDCs) have been identified in this section.

The Problems of VEDCs as Perceived by the Members

Ideally speaking, the VEDC is a platform created at the village level to facilitate the solutions of the day to day problems encountered by the village school. It is a mechanism provided to the community people to participate in the school related activities so as to establish a problem-free facilitating teaching-learning environment at the grass roots level. But ironically, these bodies rather than solving the problems of the school are themselves fraught with problems of varied nature that impede their effective

Table 7.6: The Problems of the VEDCs as perceived by members

Sl. No.	Problems	Distribution of Respondents (Yes Response)						
		Head teachers	Panchayat members	PTA members	Ex-Military Personnel	Retired Teachers	Ph'pists/ NRIs	Total
1.	Lack of interest of members in the functioning of VEDC	41 (78.8)	85 (82.5)	80 (78.4)	38 (73.1)	39 (76.5)	36 (70.6)	319 (77.6)
2.	Members do not attend meetings	47 (90.4)	93 (90.3)	87 (85.3)	46 (88.5)	44 (86.3)	41 (80.4)	358 (87.1)
3.	Members don't value their roles and responsibilities towards VEDC	28 (53.8)	56 (54.4)	51 (50.0)	29 (55.8)	30 (58.8)	30 (58.8)	224 (54.5)
4.	Groupism among members of community	36 (69.2)	65 (63.1)	63 (61.8)	29 (55.8)	27 (52.9)	30 (58.8)	250 (60.8)
5.	Members are usually from rich families while students from poor families	37 (71.2)	79 (76.7)	82 (80.4)	43 (82.7)	41 (80.4)	43 (84.3)	325 (79.1)
6.	Selection process of members is not objective and transparent	17 (32.7)	42 (40.8)	32 (31.4)	16 (30.8)	10 (19.6)	15 (29.4)	132 (32.1)
7.	No Incentives to members	24 (46.2)	51 (49.5)	43 (42.2)	20 (38.5)	12 (23.5)	20 (39.2)	170 (41.4)
8.	Head Teacher/Secretary is overburdened	52 (100)	64 (62.1)	64 (62.7)	29 (55.8)	26 (51.0)	29 (56.9)	264 (64.2)
Total		52 (100)	103 (100)	102 (100)	52 (100)	51 (100)	51 (100)	411 (100)

Multiple Response Table.
Source: Sample Survey.
Figures in parentheses denote percentages.

functioning. The survey elucidates that one of the major problems as perceived by 87.1 per cent members of the VEDC is regarding the attendance in VEDC meetings. As pointed out earlier that the meetings of the VEDCs are not held in first place or if at all they are held, then the VEDCs members don't come to attend the same. The signatures of the members on the minutes are obtained from their residences by the secretary. The paper work is completed to escape the disciplinary action. More than 90.4 per cent head teachers were apparently concerned about the lack of attendance/ non participation of the members in the meetings. The proportion of other members like the panchayat (90.3%), ex-servicemen (88.5%), retired teachers (86.3%) and PTA members (85.3%) in this regard was also very high. But unfortunately inspite of the concern shown by VEDCs members, they were not eager or appeared motivated to attend the meetings in future as well. Here lies an immense scope of intervention to sensitize the VEDC members towards their social commitment and involvement in the improvement of the school.

Second problem as perceived by the VEDC members was relating to composition of the VEDC. It may be highlighted here that as per the government guidelines, any individual can become the member of this body irrespective of whether his/her children study in the same school or not. This is a serious flaw as highlighted by 79.1 per cent members. As a result of this, the nominations of the members remain confined to those families who are rich and powerful and whose children necessarily are not enrolled in the same school. This is an unfortunate contradiction because it is usual that a parent whose children are not enrolled in the same school may not be as committed or concerned as the parents whose children are enrolled. Therefore, the respondents highlighted the need to restructure the composition of VEDCs so that the nominations to the VEDCs should be only of those parents whose children study in the same school. Thus it is suggested that only those individuals should be nominated to the VEDC whose children are enrolled in the same school.

During the course of field work it was also observed that a great majority of VEDC members carried an impression that VEDCs can hardly be helpful in improving the standard of education of the government school in rural areas. This impression was all pervading even across the non members as well. Maximum people believed that the VEDCs are mainly meant for construction of school buildings, toilets and rooms. During the discussions it was found that there was a general lack of the feeling of belongingness and responsibility among the community people towards the government school. People did not seem to own the village school as much as they did for a religious organization such as a mandir or a gurudwara. Statistically, 77.6 per cent VEDC members reported that there is a general lack of interest in the members in school related activities which is why the VEDCs don't function as they should. The study finds that lack of interest is serious problem that necessitates attitudinal reorientation of the members as also of the community. This is indeed a huge task as the new habits of behaviour and thinking cannot be imbibed in people in a fast forward mode. Changing the long practiced behaviour and mind set of the people take time. But nevertheless, not withstanding difficulties, efforts should be made to build a positive perception among the community people so that they proactively participate in the school activities.

Another issue that put great impediment in proper functioning of VEDCs is the unreasonable burden over the head teacher who in his capacity as head teacher has to act as the secretary of the VEDC. He remains preoccupied with one or the other work relating to this body and at the sometime, has to deal with all other issues of the children and the general administration of the school. As per the guidelines, the head teacher is entrusted with all the responsibilities ranging from nominations of VEDC members to maintaining the accounts and records of this body. He has to convene the meetings, record the minutes and not only this, he is the one who has to compile and submit all the progress reports to the appropriate authorities all by himself. The guidelines clearly mention that it is the sole responsibility of the member secretary to maintain the accounts and get all SSA work and ensure that the activities are completed as per norms. From the discussions, it was clear that the burden on head teacher is, in fact, too much and there is an urgency to unburden him by providing a helping hand. Surprisingly all the head teachers expressed serious concern over the extra workload on them. Overall, 64.2 per cent VEDC members stated that the secretary/head teacher is over-burdened which adversely affect not only the working of VEDC but also the teaching at the school as such.

Another problem highlighted by more than three-fifth (60.8%) members was the groupism among the community people. According to them getting nominated to the VEDC is viewed as a matter of prestige and the nominated member is perceived to gain power and a status change in the community. This result into a situation of competition between the groups perceived as gaining power and those that are perceived as losing power. A feeling of threat and conflict gets generated between these groups. The nomination to VEDC is, in fact, perceived by one group as eliminating or diminishing its power over the other. This competition as who stands to gain power and who doesn't, adversely affects the overall process of community involvement in the form of Village Education Development Committees. This situation demands tactical judgments of the nominating authorities to observe and grapple with the distribution and dynamics of power relations of the community people. The head teacher or the PTA of the village should hear and understand the people' perceptions before making nominations to this committee. Educating and persuading is to be emphasized and the differences are to be deemphasized to strike a balance between the dissenting and consenting groups because community participation is a collaborative process and thus requires shared understanding. This approach may possibly result in effecting the intended results but nevertheless nothing can be said with certainty about the situations involving human beings.

Yet another problem highlighted by the VEDC members was relating to the selection process of members. 32.1 per cent members viewed the selection process as subjective where caste considerations played a significant role. For more than two-fifth (41.4%) VEDC members lack of financial incentives to VEDCs members was as issue that acted as a de-motivator for the members to actively involve with the school activities.

Overall, it is clear from the analysis that there are many impediments in the smooth functioning of the VEDCs which require immediate attention of the appropriate authorities and various stakeholders. As per the findings of the study by Nayak(2009) major problems of SMCs in Orissa were inadequacy of teachers, poverty of members, lack of sufficient funds, lack of coordination among members, inadequacy of classrooms, lack of incentives for SMC members and political interference. In the light of the above and with a view to provide some concrete suggestions, the present study has attempted to solicit the opinions of the VEDCs members on ways and means by which the functioning of VEDCs can be improved.

Suggestions as Prescribed by the VEDCs Members

It is well recognized fact that people' involvement in school education cannot be orchestrated by a uniform prescription. Every programme or suggestion seeking improvement in the functioning of VEDCs has to be contextualized as per the local conditions and needs of the particular committee. Thus it is highly unlikely that the suggestions as prescribed by the present sample of respondents can be uniformly applicable across all the committees. But nevertheless many of these suggestions can help lay a roadmap for further planning and policy formulation for community participation in school education. Against the foregoing arguments some of the suggestions are being discussed here.

From the data it is evident that an overwhelming majority (92.2%) of the VEDCs members were of the view that there is a need for some financial incentives or rewards for the members for their contribution to the school related activities. These incentives or rewards, according to them, can be helpful in providing positive motivation to them. Another issue about which the members seemed greatly concerned was the involvement of teachers in non academic activities. It was pointed out by more than 81.5 per cent members that the school teachers, most of the times, have to get involved in the activities (other than teaching and learning) like the management of mid day meals or attending seminars or carrying *dak* (official correspondence) from the school to the other offices and vice versa. Apart from that, the school teachers are too frequently involved in doing surveys of the government or put on various duties such as the elections. The members suggested that involvement of teachers in non academic activities should be minimized to the extent possible or the government should appoint some non teaching staff in each school so that the burden of teachers can be shared and reduced. This way the teaches can be involved with VEDCs in a better way. This view was expressed by 94.2 per cent head teachers and 82.4 per cent PTA members.

Table 7.7: Suggestions of the VEDC members

Sl. No.	*Suggestions*	*Distribution of Respondents (Yes Response)*						
		Head teachers	*Panchayat members*	*PTA members*	*Ex-Military Personnel*	*Retired Teachers*	*Ph'pists/ NRIs*	*Total*
1.	Members should be educated	42 (80.8)	80 (77.7)	82 (80.4)	39 (75.0)	46 (90.2)	42 (82.4)	331 (80.5)
2.	Only parents whose children attend the school, be made the members	41 (78.8)	78 (75.7)	75 (73.5)	39 (75.0)	39 (76.5)	36 (70.6)	308 (74.9)
3.	Teacher should not be involved in non academic activities	49 (94.2)	81 (78.6)	84 (82.4)	37 (71.2)	40 (78.4)	44 (86.3)	335 (81.5)
4.	There should be some incentive/rewards for members	51 (98.1)	93 (90.3)	92 (90.2)	47 (90.4)	47 (92.2)	49 (96.1)	379 (92.2)
5.	VEDC members must have effective periodic trainings	38 (73.1)	80 (77.7)	74 (72.5)	40 (76.9)	38 (74.5)	36 (70.6)	306 (74.5)
6.	Secretary should be given some helping hand	52 (100)	57 (55.3)	53 (52.0)	32 (61.5)	32 (62.7)	30 (60.0)	256 (62.4)
Total		52 (100)	103 (100)	102 (100)	52 (100)	51 (100)	51 (100)	411 (100)

Multiple Response Table
Source: Sample Survey
Figures in parentheses denote percentages

Another suggestion prescribed by all the head teachers was regarding unburdening the head teacher/secretary of the VEDC. Overall, 62.4 per cent VEDC members shared this concern and pointed out that all the work of the VEDC is done by the head teacher single handedly. In fact it is true as has been pointed out earlier as well that the guidelines makes it mandatory for the secretary to carry out all the work ranging from nominations to record keeping and maintaining the accounts. Therefore, in the line of the suggestions of the VEDC members, the study recommends that in order to improve the overall functioning of the VEDCs, it is very urgent to provide some helping hand to the secretary of this body. Another suggestion as furnished by a little less than three fifth (74.9%) respondents was about restructuring the composition of the VEDCs.

As discussed in the preceding section also that only those individuals be nominated to the VEDCs whose children are enrolled in the same school. This means that the parents whose children study in other schools should be rendered ineligible for nominations. This way, the VEDCs members are more likely to display genuine concern and a sense of ownership to the school. About 80.5 per cent respondents were of the view that the community people who are educated and aware about the importance of community involvement be nominated as far as possible. This can further improve the quality of interaction between the teachers and the parents leading to a more positive and collaborative relationship between them. This aspect was highlighted by more than 90 per cent retired teachers besides 82.4 per cent philanthropists/NRIs and 80.8 per cent head teachers. The field investigation also revealed that effective periodic training of the VEDC members is the need of the hour as felt by a little less than three fourth (74.5%) respondents. As per the guidelines, periodic trainings are an important component for capacity building of VEDCs members, however, the observation revealed that hardly any training on regular basis is held for the VEDC members.

Community Participation: The Views of the Teachers

This section compiles the views of the teachers about the selected aspects of the overall working of the Village Education Development Committees. To know the opinion of the teachers, a separate interview schedule was designed and administered on the teachers to explore only the selected issues of the community participation in school education. In all, a total of 99 teachers teaching in the sampled schools were chosen randomly for knowing the views of teachers regarding overall functioning of Village Education Development Committees.

General Impression of the Teachers about the VEDCs

In order to know the general impression of the teachers about the VEDCs, following four questions were asked from them:

a) Do the VEDCs indeed contribute towards the improvement of schools?
b) Do you think the formation of VEDCs would help improve the school education?
c) Are the VEDCs useful in realizing the objectives of the Sarva Shiksha Abhiyan?
d) Do the members of VEDCs value the importance of community participation in school education?

The responses to the above mentioned questions have been analyzed on a three point scale namely: not at all, to some extent and very much. The data elucidates that only a little more than one tenth (12.1%) teachers held the optimistic view about the contribution of VEDCs towards the improvement of schools at community level while a little more than one-fourth (26.3%) teachers were on the opposite side and replied that the VEDCs absolutely don't contribute anything, whatsoever, towards the school improvement. The rest (61.6%) teachers were of the view that the contribution of the VEDCs in improvement of school cannot be ignored and these bodies certainly do have a significant role in improving overall academic environment in the school. From the analysis, it can be suggested that the general impression about the VEDCs is that they can contribute significantly towards the improvement of school education. This opinion can further be substantiated by the findings of the study by Shankar (2008) who found that VECs have a significant role to play at the grassroots level. Similarly Dash and Panda (2009) concludes that the role of VECs is very essential and important for school improvement.

However, that is not happening. In response to the second query of whether the formation of VEDCs would help improve the school education, more than one fourth (25.3%) teachers replied in affirmative and were of the view that the VEDCs provide a platform to the parents to decide about the kind of education their children should get. Through this committee, the parents can exercise their rights, express their views and participate in the decision making processes of the school education. But all that can happen only if the parents are proactive and cohesive on education related issues of their community. Further it is revealed that the percentage of the teachers who rejected the very idea of formation of VEDCs was about 17.2 per cent while about 57.6 per cent of them were somewhere in the middle of the scale indicating that they neither rejected the formation of VEDCs nor did they held a very optimistic view that the formation of VEDCs would solve all the school related problems. But nonetheless they agreed that the VEDCs can be helpful to a great extent in enhancing the quality of school education at the community level. As regards the usefulness of VEDCs in realizing the goals of SSA, more than 90 per cent teachers held a positive opinion. The teachers who held at a negative view on this aspect were very less (8.1%).

Table 7.8 General Impression of Teachers about VEDCs

Sl. No.	*Indicators*	*Distribution of Respondents (Yes Response)*			*Total*
		Not at All	*To Some Extent*	*Very Much*	
1.	Do the VEDCs indeed contribute towards the improvement of schools?	26 (26.3)	61 (61.6)	12 (12.1)	99 (100)
2.	Do you think the formation of VEDC would help improve the school education?	17 (17.2)	57 (57.6)	25 (25.3)	99 (100)
3.	Is the VEDC useful in realizing the objectives of Sarva Shiksha Abhiyan?	8 (8.1)	72 (72.7)	19 (19.2)	99 (100)
4.	Do the VEDC members value the importance of community participation in elementary education?	49 (49.5)	40 (40.4)	10 (10.1)	99 (100)

Multiple Response Table.
Source: Sample Survey.
Figures in parentheses denote percentages.

It can be seen from the analysis that nearly one fifth (19.2%) teachers were highly optimistic while about three fourth (72.7%) agreed that VEDCs to some extent have a role in realizing the goals of the SSA provided the community people are sensitized and mobilized towards importance of their involvement in achieving universal enrollment, retention and equity with regard to education for all. Same thing has been emphasized by Nayak (2009) who is of the opinion that community participation in management of primary education is indispensible and inevitable in materializing the goals of universalisation of primary education. Dash and Panda (2009) concludes that the function of community is proved to be very effective in all kinds of school related activities. The analysis of teachers' responses about the members of VEDCs valuing the importance of community participation in school education depicts that nearly half (49.5%) of them were of the view that VEDCs members not at all attach any importance to community participation. That is one of the primary reasons why the quality of education in rural areas is very poor. According to these teachers there is a total disconnect between school and community and the onus of it lies on the community people only. If the community people have a sense of ownership for the school just as they do for religious institutions, it would definitely enhance the educational outcomes. Further about one tenth (10.1%) teachers were of the opinion that the VEDCs members do give importance to community participation in school related activities.

Teachers' Satisfaction about Performance of VEDCs

In this section, it has been attempted to know the extent of satisfaction of teachers on selected aspects of the working of VEDCs namely the performance with regard to increasing enrollment, reducing dropout, improving school result and issues relating to infrastructure, resources and grants. The analysis has been done on a three point scale: satisfied, somewhat satisfied, not at all satisfied.

The data revealed that the teachers did not appear to be fully satisfied with the performance of VEDCs as regards the expected educational outcomes from these bodies. Only 8.1 per cent teachers expressed satisfaction with regards their role to increase the enrollment while more than two fifth (40.4%) were not at all satisfied on this aspect. Maximum teachers (82.8%) were dissatisfied over the performance of VEDCs towards monitoring of teachers' attendance in the school. These teachers accepted that fact that many teachers remain absent from duty on one or the other pretext and there is no effective monitoring mechanism in place except the community people in the form of VEDCs. But unfortunately the VEDCs don't show any commitment and sincerity to ensure the attendance of teachers in the respective schools.

Though some of the VEDCs members, at times, do interact with teachers in their individual capacity on this issue but the issue, as such, is not formally taken up as the agenda item for the VEDCs meetings. The teachers suggested that the VEDCs must work cohesively and unitedly and should hold meetings to discuss about the difficulties usually faced by the teachers. The data further depicted that the satisfaction was maximum with regard to performance of VEDCs in relation to utilization of grants (41.4%) and creation of infrastructural facilities (40.4%). These findings reinforce the fact that the major role that the VEDCs play in the school activities relate to the utilization of grants and infrastructural activities. Otherwise than these two aspects, the satisfaction level of teachers about the contribution of VEDCs was very low. It was, in fact, the lowest for their performance towards the improvement in school results (5.1%) and the monitoring of teachers' attendance (3.0%). The dissatisfaction of teachers was the highest on these two aspects only.

Activities of VEDCs: Views of Teachers

This section takes into account various activities undertaken by the VEDCs from the point of teachers. This was considered useful in getting an idea about the variations in the responses of teachers and the VEDCs members. The analysis has been done on the individual activities of the members and the activities performed by the VEDCs as a body in terms of improving school infrastructure, fundraising and activities undertaken for improving general academic environment of the school.

Individual contribution of VEDCs members: Views of Teachers

The data reflected that there was a marked difference between the views of the teachers and the members of the VEDCs. As regards the members paying visits to the school for monitoring and inspection of teachers' attendance in school, only one-tenth (10.1%) teachers (as against 22.4 per cent VEDCs members) replied in affirmative while the rest about 90 per cent of teachers were of the opinion that the members do not visit schools at all. Further 35.4 per cent teachers in comparison to 39.4 per cent VEDC members were of the view that the members do participate and contribute to organization of school functions. The findings of the study by Nayak (2002) found that 54.16 per cent VEC members visited the school regularly and made efforts at their level to ensure the regular attendance of children in the schools in Orissa. In answer to the query whether the VEDC members discuss the problems of school at appropriate quarters, a little more than one-tenth (11.2%) teachers as against 20 per cent VEDC members replied in the affirmative. From the information, it can be inferred that the individual contribution of members with regard to holding discussions with appropriate officials of the government was very poor while at the same time their contribution towards arranging funds/donations for the school was also very dissatisfactory from the point of view of teachers as just 8.1 per cent teachers (as against 44 per cent VEDCs members) had a positive opinion on this aspect. With regard to members-teachers interaction, the difference between the views of teachers and the members was very pronounced as it was 18.2 per cent teachers as against 35.8 per cent members who agreed that the members-teachers interaction do take place once a while. From this, it can be suggested that although the member-teacher interaction do take place but there is a need to make the interaction more focused and qualitative.

Overall, the views of the teachers about the contribution of members in their individual capacity were not very inspiring and positive and thus there is a need for sensitization of VEDC members so that they can be more proactive towards enhancing the educational outcomes at the school level.

Activities of VEDCs: Views of Teachers

As has already been pointed out earlier that the VEDCs undertake mostly those activities which are essential under government guidelines and the avoidance of which entail disciplinary action, the same view was expressed by the teachers as well. Maximum (82.8%) teachers agreed that the VEDCs are involved in carrying out the activities relating to construction and maintenance to fulfill various procedural requirements. The teachers emphasized that whatever the VEDCs do is only on papers. In actual practice, it is the head teacher and not the VEDC that does everything. Once the work like constructing a room etc is complete, the head teacher gets the signatures from VEDCs members for completing the official requirement. The contribution of VEDCs, as such, is only marginal. About 9.1 per cent teachers as against 12.7 per cent VEDC members agreed that the VEDCs did carry out some fundraising activities but the fundraising activities were undertaken by the individual members only. The VEDCs in a formal sense did not launch any such drive at the village level. As regards the incentives to the girls/SC students, 56.6 per cent teachers were of the view that VEDCs involve in implementation of the incentives and schemes launched by the government for students' welfare like the free text books/notebooks, exposure visits and vocational courses etc. However this involvement was not very well organized. Only a few members rather than the whole committee extended a helping hand to the head teacher. Here it may be highlighted that a little more than one tenth (10.1%) teachers mentioned that the VEDCs did undertake some activities of the general nature like making announcements, speaking to community people especially parents to enroll the out-of-children to school, putting up display boards about grants and civil works. The present analysis gives a cross-check of the contribution of VEDCs as stated by the VEDCs members and the teachers. Since the variations in the responses of the two groups are not in contrast with each other, it is an indication that the VEDCs do undertake some activities. These are mainly the activities which are essential under the government guidelines, the avoidance of which amounts to violation of the prescribed rules.

Summing up

The data indicated that in terms of availability of infrastructural facilities, the situation is reasonably good, however, the facilities in the government schools were far less than the private schools both in terms of quality as well as quality. No government school had any play facilities like a swing or a seesaw or toys for small children. Even basic sport facilities like bats, balls, nets and rackets etc. were not available to the children. Thus it is a clear indication that the government schools require more facilities than just the basic (the drinking water, rooms, toilets, ramps and electricity) to have a better and joyful learning environment and to compete with private schools. The awareness of members of VEDCs about composition, process of formation and the functions of VEDC did not reveal an inspiring scenario. The data on contribution of VEDCs indicated that the contribution of these bodies towards increasing enrollment, reducing dropout and improving school results was only marginal. The VEDCs merely do things that are essentially unavoidable under the government rules. As regards the problems being faced by these bodies, it is clear that the major problems as indicated by the VEDCs member were relating to the lack of interest among the members in school related activities apart from their non-participation in the meetings. The teachers did not appear to be satisfied with the performance of VEDCs in their respective schools. The views of teachers reinforced the belief that the contribution of VEDCs is much less than the desired level. In general, the functioning of the VEDCs was not very impressive and there are miles to go to achieve the mandate of community participation for effective implementation of Sarva Shiksha Abhiyan.

8

Witnessing the Present for Capturing the Future

Sarva Shiksha Abhiyan (SSA) launched in the year 2002, aims to Universalize Elementary Education (UEE) through people's involvement and participation. SSA assigns greatest importance to systematic mobilization of the community and creation of an effective system of decentralized decision making. It calls for community ownership of school-based interventions through effecting decentralization. It puts a great deal of emphasis on the civil society for ensuring the effectiveness and viability of our school education. Institutions such as Village Education Committee/School Management and Development Committee/ Ward Education Committees have been set up at village or school level in almost all the states to ensure community participation in the school education system. The Right to Education Act 2009 is another historic step which recognizes the role of local governance in school education. The Act specifies that a School Management Committee (SMC) shall be constituted for every school to monitor and oversee its working, and to plan and facilitate its overall development with representation of parents, teachers and community and local authority members, as may be prescribed by the appropriate State government.

As such community participation in education through Village Educational Committees has been given utmost importance in most policy documents of the Government relating to school education and the crucial link between community participation and equitable quality education has always been given due recognition.

The review of related literature shows that most of the research studies relating to community participation have considered the importance of participation of community in school management without a doubt. But at the same time, these studies also accept the fact there are many factors that act as impediments in the path of achieving a more inclusive and equitable school education through Village Education Committees. Menon (1999) reiterates that the women still observed *purdah* and many of them do not even look up to male members and speak in Haryana. Tyagi (1999) while studying Village Education Committees in Ranchi District revealed VEDC members do not attend the meetings regularly and also not taking part in any school activities. Government of Karnataka (2004) in collaboration with Azim Premji Foundation found that 2 per cent of the schools in Karnataka didn't even have a School Development and Management Committee. The monitoring mechanism seemed to be ineffective. There was low representation of girls as student representatives in SDMCs. Mor (2008) points out that the quality issues have no place in VEDCs meetings in Punjab. A great majority of VEDCs/PTAs and gram sabhas don't have education on their priority list. VEDCs members did not even attend the meetings. Those who attended did the same just to complete formality and had no interest in quality issue of elementary education. Nayak (2009) finds that the working of the SMCs in Orissa was not at all satisfactory. The meetings are either not held at all or, if held, they are just once in a year. The SMC members did not attend the SMC meetings whenever they are held. Various problems perceived as impediments in the working of the SMCs were inadequacy of teachers, poverty of members, lack of sufficient financial aids, lack of coordination among members, inadequacy of classrooms, lack of incentives for SMC members, political interference and reservation of SMC seats in the village community. Interestingly gender of the chairman of SMC was perceived to be important for the effective functioning of these bodies. The study by Institute of Rural Research and Development (2010) reveals that more than half of the VEC members in Mewat in Haryana are inadequately informed about their roles and responsibilities. Their participation in activities to ensure quality formal education in the villages is also inadequate. The members admitted to having received no formal training, before being made members of VEC. Aikara (2011) while studying the decentralization of elementary education and community participation in Kerala stressed that decentralization of education in Kerala has not resulted in greater participation of the stakeholders like teachers and parents in school management. There is a need for more convergence of state support and the social capital of the civil society. The major aspects of school education are with the centralized state department of education.

On the whole, most of the research studies make is clear that mere presence of a VEC in a village may not transform the educational scenario so long as the members of these committees are not active and sensitized. It is very important to understand how these committees can work more effectively, what mechanisms and strategies should be used and what are the expectations and perception of the people about the whole process and how can they be made more proactive about their involvement in the school related activities at the village level. In this context, the research study has primarily intended to evaluate the functioning of Village Education Development Committees in the state of Punjab. The conclusions and recommendations emerging from the empirical data are being presented in the subsequent section.

Formation, Composition and Functions

The study found that the composition of all the VEDCs and formation of the VEDCs was according to the Guidelines prescribed by the Sarva Shiksha Abhiyan Authority of the Government of Punjab. However the VEDCs members had varied perceptions about their functions. According to more three fourth VEDC members, the main function of VEDCs was stated to be to undertake civil/construction and maintenance work in the school while more than two-fifth were of the view that the VEDCs have to assist in proper utilization of grants/funds received from the government from time to time for the development of the school. An almost equal proportion was of the opinion that the major functions of these committees are to identify the needs and problems of the school.

Socio-Demographic Profile of VEDC Members

The presence of women as members of the VEDCs was bare minimum as in all the VEDCs in the present sample, the number of women was only up to the extent to which it met the mandatory requirement of the Government Guidelines. The study concludes the entry of women into VEDCs is mainly due to the mandatory provision of having at least two women as VEDC members (out of the total eight) provided in the Government Guidelines. The VEDCs, by and large, remain a male bastion and the personal merit of woman remains overshadowed by the patriarchal stereotypes and culture factors adverse to gender equality.

Age

The study finds that 45.3 per cent respondents were in the age group of 45-60 years and 18.7 per cent respondents were in the age group of 60 years and above. This clearly indicates that 64 per cent VEDCs members were older than 45 years of age. The findings establish the fact that the older people continue to outnumber the younger people in Punjab as far as the participation in the school related issues is concerned. The survey clearly indicates that age still remains an important criterion in determining the leadership positions in rural areas particularly in the school related activities. The VEDCs in Punjab continue to be dominated by the not so young people.

Level of Education

The analysis revealed that just 08 of the total 411 respondents (1.9%) were illiterate while the rest of them had formal education ranging from primary level to post graduation level. Among the educated respondents, 28.7 per cent VEDCs members were graduates while 10 per cent were post graduates, nearly one-fourth (22.6%) of them had passed higher secondary while 29.7 per cent were matriculates. This means that the VEDCs members in the present sample were fairly educated as more than 90 per cent of the total members had formal educational qualifications higher than matriculation.

Castes/Category

Nearly three-fifth (59.4%) members belonged to general castes followed by the scheduled castes (31.1%). Nearly one-tenth (9.5%) members belonged to the other backward castes groups. From the analysis it is clear that the VEDCs are primarily dominated by the people from the general castes. This is mainly because of the absence of caste-based provisions of reservation for VEDC memberships in the Guidelines of the State Government. Though the Guidelines mentions that tnere must be reasonable representation of all the castes residing in a village community, the people of dominant castes continue to form the bulk of leadership positions in rural areas, at least, as far as the membership to VEDCs is concerned. Thus it is concluded that in absence of specific reservation provisions, the people of dominant castes tend to monopolize the leadership positions with reference to community participation in the school related activities.

Marital Status

The study finds that a huge majority (97.3%) of the VEDC members were married while only a few (2.7%) were unmarried. The findings reinforce the argument that the marital status of an individual certainly has a positive role in the process of acquiring leadership roles in villages like the membership to a Village Education Development Committee at the community level. The marriage as an institution certainly provides an enlarged social space to an individual in the rural communities.

Availability of Facilities in Schools

As regards the school building, it was found that there was no school in the sample without a building or a school housed in a *kucha* building. All the school buildings were owned by the government and nearly 90 per cent school buildings were in a fairly good condition, but very poorly maintained. They are not properly white-washed or painted on regular basis. About 17.3 per cent school buildings did not need any repair whereas significantly three-fifth (75%) school buildings required one or the other minor repair work. However, there was no school whose building was found to be in dilapidated condition and nor there was any school whose building paused a danger to the life of the teachers and the students. The study underlines that the VEDCs can certainly play as important role in proper maintenance and upkeep of the school buildings in the villages.

The study finds that all schools in District Muktsar and Mansa had drinking water facilities whereas 96.2 per cent schools in Mansa and 100 per cent schools of District Muktsar had girls' toilets. In total 98.1 per cent schools in the sample had girls' toilets within the school premises. As regards the availability of a proper electricity connection in the school, the analysis revealed that there were a little more than one-third (36.5%) schools in the sample which had a government approved electric connection.

As regards the availability of chairs to teachers, the situation was good as all the schools had chairs for the teachers. The tables to teachers were not available in about one-fifth schools. So far as the availability of benches to students is concerned, the situation was very unsatisfactory as in about three-fourth schools; there were no benches for the students. In these schools, the students either sat on mats provided by the school or they carried their own mats (fertilizer bags) along with them. The present study finds that the participation of VEDCs members in maintenance, upkeep and the purchase of furniture was minimal. All the arrangements were being made by the head teacher alone. The VEDCs are expected to ensure more cooperation towards upkeep and maintenance of furniture in the schools.

About 3.8 per cent schools in the sample did not have boundary walls. Nearly one-fifth (19.2%) schools in the sample did not have an open space worth playing for children. No school had manpower for maintaining the playgrounds nor were there any sport facilities like the balls, nets, rackets etc. In about 9.6 per cent schools there were no library/book banks. First aids kits were not available in about 2 per cent schools. About 7.7 per cent schools did not even have a wall clock.

The analysis shows that the things like black boards, chalks, dusters, almirahs/boxes, school bells and mid day meals were available in all the schools but the quality and the maintenance of these facilities required immediate attention. The study underlines that apart from the availability, what is more important is the proper care and maintenance of the facilities by the appropriate stakeholders.

The study finds that there is an utter lack of will and involvement of the community in the processes of school governance like micro planning and preparing habitation plans etc.

The study underlines the urgency to further improve the school infrastructure so as to make it at par with the private schools. Secondly the human factor in terms of teacher' characteristics and the community people should also be focused upon. The focus of attention needs to be both on the infrastructural facilities as well as the characteristics of teachers and the parents. Unless this paradigm shift take place, it is highly unlikely that the government schools would have any visible impact on the quality of education at the grassroots level. It is high time that the government bring some radical changes in the school education apparatus itself like the appointment of good teachers and strict monitoring mechanisms for truants and shirkers.

The Awareness of the Members

As regards the awareness of the VEDCs members about the Composition of the VEDC it was found that about one-third (32.1%) respondents were fully aware about the Composition while only 5.1 per cent respondents were not at all aware about it. A huge chunk of more than three fifth (62.8%) respondents were in between i.e. neither were fully aware nor were absolutely ignorant about the Composition of the VEDCs. Overall, the awareness of VEDCs members to an extent of 32.1 per cent respondents being fully aware while 62.8 per cent being partially aware present a fairly good scenario. Nevertheless, the study underlines that the awareness and thereby the performance of the members of VEDCs can further be improved by providing regular periodic trainings to the VEDC members on this aspect. The respondents who were in the middle category of awareness (partially aware) can certainly be made to cross over to the first category (fully aware) provided they are given proper knowledge inputs by way of organizing some lecture/seminar/workshops etc. at the school level.

As regards the awareness regarding the process of Formation, about 17.3 per cent of the members of the VEDC did not know anything about the procedure followed for nominating various members while a little less than one-third (29.0%) respondents were fully aware and 53.8 per cent were partially aware about the process of formation of VEDCs.

From the analysis, it is suggested that there is a possibility of sharing more information with the VEDCs members on the procedures followed for formation of this Committee. As majority of the members were in the middle category of awareness scale i.e. partially aware, the study underlines the urgency of motivating this chunk so as to enable them to cross over to the fully aware category of awareness. The information sharing coupled with motivation can possibly lead to more involvement of the members in the school related activities, thereby, improving the functioning of the committees.

In order to know the awareness level of the VEDC on whether the membership to VEDCs is determined by nomination or election, 72.5 per cent were of the view that the members to the VEDC are nominated rather than elected. There were just 2.7 per cent respondents who replied that the membership is determined through elections while unexpectedly 24.8 per cent expressed ignorance on this aspect. As regards the awareness of members about as to who nominates whom, nearly three-fifth (59.6%) respondents knew that the panchayat members are nominated by the village panchayat, 68.6 per cent knew that the PTA members are nominated by the PTA. The PTA also nominates the retired teacher was known correctly by 66.7 per cent respondents. 34.8 per cent respondents knew that philanthropist/NRI is nominated by the DEO (Elementary Education) on recommendations from the head teacher.

From the findings it is inferred that although the respondents were reasonably aware about the fact that the nominations is the principle criterion for determination of VEDC membership, however, the awareness on as to who nominate whom was relatively less. Saying more generally, the actual procedure adopted for determining the membership was not very well known by the members.

As regards the awareness about Functions, only a little more than one-fourth (25.8%) respondents replied that they were fully aware about the functions of this body whereas 70.8 per cent were partially aware and 3.4 per cent respondents were totally ignorant about the functions. The findings suggested that the members of the VEDCs need more information on the functions. This can be done through periodic trainings or awareness lectures by appropriate officials of the Government.

The VEDCs members mainly perceived VEDCs as the bodies meant to undertake the construction/civil works and for carrying out activities relating to the utilization of grants or organizing social functions/celebrations at the school level. The study underlines the need of changing this general perception and make the members realize that VEDCs are the people' forum made to encourage community participation in school activities so as to improve the quality of educational services by performing functions of a varied nature and not just the functions relating to utilization of grants/funds and organizing the cultural programmes. Ironically, no member (except Secretaries) in the sample perceived VEDCs as a community owned institution made to achieve better standards of school education at the grassroots level.

The Contribution of Village Education Development Committees

Increasing Enrollment

The analysis suggested before the formation of VEDCs in the high literacy villages, the gross enrollment increased by 0.51 per cent during the year 2000-01 and 2001-02 and by 2.10 per cent during the second year (2001-02 to 2002-03). After the formation of VEDCs, the gross enrollment increased by 2.25 per cent during 2003-04 and 2004-05 while by 11.46 per cent during 2004-05 and 2005-06. This shows that the rate of increase in the gross enrollment in the high literacy villages was higher after the formation of the VEDCs in comparison to the period of two years when VEDCs were not in place. Thus it can be said that the Village Education Development Committees contributed positively towards the rate of increase in the gross enrollment in the high literacy regions. Across gender, the VEDCs had a positive contribution towards increasing girls' gross enrollment as well as boys' gross enrollment in the high literacy regions.

In the low literacy regions, before the formation of VEDCs, there was a decrease of 5.03 per cent during the year 2000-01 and 2001-02 whereas in the following year (from 2001-02 to 2002-03), the enrollment increased by 3.54 per cent. After the formation of the VEDCs, the gross enrollment dropped by 2.72 per cent during the first year (2003-04 to 2004-05) and by 3.13 per cent in the following year (2004-05 to 2005-06). Thus from the findings it is concluded that the formation of VEDCs did not make any significant contribution with regard to the increase in enrollment of students in the low literacy villages. Across the gender similar pattern was followed. Thus it is concluded that VEDCs did not have any role across gender of students.

Improving School Results

In high literacy villages, before the formation of VEDCs, the number of failures declined by 42.33 per cent during the year 2000-01 and 2001-02 while the number of failures increased by 62.02 per cent during the year 2001-02 and 2002-03 while after formation of the VEDCs, the number of failures increased by 24.27 per cent in year 2003-04 and 2004-05 while it decreased by 11.7 per cent during 2004-05 and 2005-06. Thus from the findings it is suggested that the VEDCs did not play any role in improving the school results in the high literacy villages.

In the low literacy regions, before the formation of VEDCs, the number of failures increased by 1.29 per cent during 2000-01 and 2001-02 and by 5.73 per cent during 2001-02 and 2002-03. After the VEDCs were formed, there was a drop of 56.7 per cent in the number of failures during 2003-04 and 2004-05 and further a drop of 22.89 per cent was witnessed during 2004-05 and 2005-06. Thus it is suggested that since the school results have improved after the formation of VEDCs in the low literacy regions, the VEDCs has played a positive role towards reducing the number of failures thus improving the school results.

Reducing Dropout

In high literacy villages, before formation of VEDCs, the dropout rate has decreased by 16.67 per cent during 2000-01 and 2001-02 and by 34.28 per cent during 2001-02 and 2002-03. After the formation of the VEDCs, the drop out increased by 196.7 per cent during 2003-04 and 2004-05 and there was a decrease of 65.21 per cent during 2004-05 and 2005-06. This means that the VEDCs did not play any positive role in reduction of dropout rate in the high literacy villages.

In the low literacy villages, before the formation of the VEDCs, the dropout rate has witnessed an increase of 57.14 per cent from 2000-01 to 2001-02 whereas the dropout rate decreased by 32.72 per cent during 2001-02 and 2002-03. After the VEDCs were formed, the dropout rate increased by 105.17 per cent during 2003-04 and 2004-05 and it got reduced by 35.25 per cent during 2004-05 and 2005-06. From the findings it is suggested that the VEDCs did not play any significant role in reducing the school dropout rate in the sampled schools situated in the low literacy villages.

Contribution of VEDCs Members in Individual Capacity

The findings revealed that only about one-fifth (20.0%) members discussed the problems of the school with the appropriate officials or the parents while a little more than one-fifth (22.4%) members had paid one or two visits to the school with an aim of monitoring the school environment. As regards the member-teacher interaction on issues relating to school improvement only 35.8 per cent members gave an affirmative reply. 44.0 per cent members has collected money for organizing sports activities in the school and contributed towards arranging funds/donations for the school. In general, the findings suggest that the contribution of individual members of the VEDCs with regard to school improvement has not been very encouraging except for the head teachers. Thus the study underlines the need for initiating some programme for morale boosting of the VEDCs members so that they develop a feeling of belongingness towards their school and contribute significantly in their individual capacity.

Conduct of Meetings

The present study finds that the meetings of the VEDCs are not held in accordance with the Guidelines laid down by the Sarva Shiksha Abhiyan Authority Punjab and most of the norms regarding conduct of meetings of these bodies are not followed in letter and spirit.

Number of VEDC Meetings

The meetings of the VEDCs are not at all a monthly feature. In fact, no formal meetings of the VEDCs are held. The meetings of the VEDCs are held on papers only. Whenever a grant is received, the head teacher/secretary after recording the minutes of the meeting on his own, sends the register to the residences of the VEDCs members for signatures. This way the paper formality is completed.

Attendance in VEDC Meetings

The VEDC members don't come to the school for meetings inspite of requests from the Secretary. It is the primary reason why the VEDC meetings are to be held in circulation. A huge majority (89.5%) of the VEDC members themselves agreed that they don't give any importance to the VEDC meetings as they viewed the meetings of VEDCs just as a formality. As per them, the VEDCs meetings don't serve any purpose; attending or not attending them does not make any difference. The study finds that there is a general lack of interest among the teachers as well as the VEDC members towards VEDCs. Therefore it is suggested that there is a need to reorient the VEDC members such that they begin to value the importance of VEDC meetings.

Issues Discussed in the Meetings

There are two major issues that always find a place in the minutes of the VEDC meetings. The first relate to making provisions for infrastructural facilities like construction of rooms, repair of buildings, purchase of furniture and other such civil or maintenance jobs while the second is regarding the utilization of grants. The major focus of VEDCs remains on the issues relating to financial matters. An omission in the matters involving money like not discussing them in the VEDCs meetings etc. entails serious disciplinary action. Therefore, the Secretary/head teacher is particularly careful in completing all the paper work in this regard. To escape any reprimand or punishment from the higher authorities, such issues are always recorded in the minutes of the VEDCs meetings. The quality issues like teaching learning material, classroom processes and learning achievements etc. are not considered of much worth for the meetings as avoidance of these issues don't entail any serious punishment.

Activities undertaken to In.prove Infrastructure

Majority (81.1%) of the VEDC members informed that the main activities undertaken by the VEDCs were about repairing and constructing the classrooms followed by repairing and constructing the toilets and ramps (70.4%). Nearly one-third (28.19%) respondents told that the VEDC repaired/constructed boundary wall of the school whereas a little more than one-tenth (11.1%) of these respondents informed that the Committee purchased furniture for teachers and students.

Activities for Fundraising

The VEDCs don't give any importance to fundraising activities. 87.3 per cent VEDCs members replied in the negative when asked if the VEDC had undertaken any fundraising activity in their community. About 12.7 per cent members informed that the VEDC they represent had collected donations for organizing some sports events.

Activities for Incentives to Students

The VEDCs participate only in those activities which are sponsored either by the State or the Central Government. As regards the incentives to students, 82.5 per cent VEDC members informed that the VEDCs organized exposure visits for the school children whereas 79.6 per cent respondents told that free text books/ notebooks schemes being monitored by these committees. As per 77.6 per cent respondents, the VEDCS were involved in giving cash prizes to the first three toppers of each class in every school. Other activities where the VEDCs participated related to vocational courses for girls like the course on computer literacy, embroidery and soft skills. There was no scheme/incentive known to have been launched by the VEDCs themselves i.e. by generating their own funds.

General/Miscellaneous Activities

As regards the activities of general nature, a huge majority of respondents (85.4%) were of the view that the VEDCs did not undertake any activity other than those mandated under government norms. Only about 14.6 per cent respondents told that the VEDCs they represented had undertaken one or the other activities for increasing enrollment and school results and reducing dropout. These activities were putting up of boards at various places within the village displaying the details of civil works and utilization of grants, making announcements from the gurudwaras from time to time regarding various school related issues, organizing cultural programme and sports, holding door to door meetings, organizing lectures and speaking to local activists/ community leaders about the problems at the school.

Overall, the contribution of VEDCs towards school related activities other than those mandated under SSA norms is very poor. This aspect is indicative of the lack of initiative and motivation among the VEDCs members towards school improvement. Therefore the study underlines the urgency to design some mechanisms for activating the VEDC members for a more proactive involvement in initiating new activities for quality school education.

The Problems of VEDCs

The major problem as perceived by 87.1 per cent members of the VEDC is regarding the attendance in VEDC meetings. Second problem as perceived by the VEDC members was relating to composition of the VEDC. Here it is worth highlighting that the nominations of the members remain confined to those families who are rich and powerful and whose children necessarily are not enrolled in the same school. Thus there is a need to restructure the composition of VEDCs so that the nominations to the VEDCs should be only of those parents whose children study in the same school.

Lack of interest among the community people towards the government school was yet another problem highlighted by 77.6 per cent respondents. People did not seem to own the village school as much as they did for a religious organization such as a mandir or a gurudwara. This situation necessitates attitudinal reorientation of the members as also of the community.

Another issue that put great impediment in proper functioning of VEDCs is the unreasonable burden over the head teacher as stated by 64.2 per cent VEDC members. The head teacher has to act as the secretary of the VEDC, take care of the general administration of the school besides taking classes.

Three-fifth (60.8%) members were of the view that the groupism among the community people is a serious problem in the smooth functioning of VEDCs. This situation demands tactical judgments on the part of the nominating authorities to observe and grapple with the distribution and dynamics of power relations of the community people. The head teacher or the PTA of the village should hear and understand the people' perceptions before making nominations to this committee.

For more than two-fifth (41.4%) VEDC members lack of financial incentives to VEDCs members was as issue that acted as a de-motivator for the members to actively involve with the school activities.

Suggestions

An overwhelming majority (92.2%) of the VEDCs members were of the view that there is a need for some financial incentives or rewards for the VEDC members for their contribution to the school related activities. These incentives or rewards can be helpful in providing positive motivation to them thereby strengthening the VEDCs.

Majority (81.5%) of the VEDC members suggested that the school teachers should not be involved in the activities (other than teaching and learning) like the management of mid day meals or attending seminars or carrying dak (official correspondence) from the school to the other offices and vice versa. It is suggested that the involvement of teachers in non academic activities should be minimized to the extent possible or the government should appoint some non teaching staff in each school so that the burden of teachers can be shared and reduced.

About 80.5 per cent respondents were of the view that the community people who are educated and aware about the importance of community involvement be nominated to the VEDCs as far as possible. Three fifth (74.9%) respondents suggested restructuring the composition of the VEDCs. Only those individuals should be nominated to the VEDCs whose children are enrolled in the same school. This means that the parents whose children study in other schools should be rendered ineligible for nominations.

Effective periodic training of the VEDC members on various aspects of the functioning of the VEDCs was stressed by a little less than three fourth (74.5%) respondents. More than three-fifth (62.4%) VEDC members suggested that the burden of the head teacher should be reduced or shared by others. In order to improve the overall functioning of the VEDCs, it is very urgent to provide some helping hand to the secretary of this body.

The Views of Teachers about overall Working of VEDCs

The general impression of the teachers about the VEDCs is that they can contribute significantly towards the improvement of school education. However, that is not happening. The data elucidates that only a little more than one tenth (12.1%) teachers held the optimistic view about the contribution of VEDCs towards the improvement of schools at community level while a little more than one-fourth (26.3%) teachers held the opposite view. The rest were undecided about this aspect.

More than one fourth (25.3%) teachers were of the view that the formation of VEDCs would help improve the school education. They expressed that the VEDCs provide a platform to the parents to decide about the kind of education their children should get. The percentage of the teachers who rejected the very idea of formation of VEDCs was about 17.2 per cent while about 57.6 per cent of them were somewhere in between.

One fifth (19.2%) teachers were of the opinion that that the VEDCs are very useful in realizing the goals of SSA while about three fourth (72.7%) teachers were of the view that the VEDCs are useful in realizing the goals of the SSA only upto some extent and that too when the community people are sensitized and mobilized towards realizing the importance of their involvement in school related issues like achieving universal enrollment, retention and equity with regard to education for all. Nearly half (49.5%) of the teachers were of the opinion that the members of VEDCs don't value the importance of community participation in school education and thus don't attach any importance to school related activities.

Teachers' Satisfaction about Performance of VEDCs

Maximum teachers (82.8%) were dissatisfied over the performance of VEDCs towards monitoring of teachers' attendance in the school. The satisfaction of teachers was highest with regard to performance of VEDCs in relation to utilization of grants (41.4%) and the creation of infrastructural facilities (40.4%). Satisfaction was the lowest for the performance of VEDCs towards the improvement in school results (5.1%) and the monitoring of teachers' attendance (3.0%). This reinforces that the main focus of VEDCs remain on civil works only.

Individual Contribution of VEDCs Members

The views of the teachers about the contribution of members in their individual capacity were not very inspiring and positive and thus there is a need for sensitization of VEDC members so that they can be more proactive towards enhancing the educational outcomes at the school level.

Activities of VEDCs: Views of Teachers

Maximum (82.8%) teachers agreed that the VEDCs are involved

in carrying out the activities relating to construction and maintenance to fulfill various procedural requirements. The teachers emphasized that whatever the VEDCs do is only on papers. In actual practice, it is the head teacher and not the VEDC that does everything. Once the work like constructing a room etc is complete, the head teacher gets the signatures from VEDC members for completing the official requirement. The contribution of VEDCs, as such, is only marginal.

Recommendations

The Study points to the need for improving different aspects of the functioning of the Village Education Development Committees based on the findings. The major changes needed for improving the overall working of VEDCs are ascertained below:

1. ***Restructuring of the VEDCs:*** There is a need for restructuring the composition of the VEDCs. The parents whose children are enrolled in the same school should only be nominated to VEDCs while the rest whose children study in other schools be rendered ineligible.
2. ***Determination of Memberships:*** Paradigm Shift is required for determination of membership to VEDCs. As per existing norms, the VEDC is constituted of the Panchayat members, members from PTA, Ex-servicemen, Retired teachers and Philanthropists/NRIs. The present criterion of determining membership is restricted only to the positions that the individual hold in the community i.e. one has to be either a member of panchayat or e member of PTA or a retired teacher or an ex-serviceman or a philanthropist or a NRI. There is no provision for entry of an individual who does not fall in any of the above categories or say for an individual who does not hold these positions even if someone may be a highly respectful and reputed person in the community. As such there is no weightage to the reputation that he/she enjoys in his/her community. Therefore the study recommends that individual's reputation alone should be the criterion for determining memberships to the VEDC. The nominations should be made as far as possible in the Gram Sabha

meetings in the presence of teachers and DEO (Elementary Education).

3. ***Strengthening School Infrastructure:*** The study underlines the urgency to further improve the school infrastructure so as to make it at par to that of the private schools and secondly the human factor in terms of teacher' characteristics should also be focused upon. The focus of attention needs to be both on the infrastructural facilities as well as the characteristics of teachers and the parents. Unless this paradigm shift take place, it is highly unlikely that the government schools would have any visible impact on the quality of education at the grassroots level. It is high time that the government and the community bring some radical changes in the school education apparatus itself. It is already clear that despite Punjab being at the top in school infrastructure (Education Development Index: 2011), a lot more is needed to improve the school education in terms of the quality, equity and the parity with the private schools.
4. ***Providing Incentives or Rewards to VEDC Members:*** The VEDC members should be provided some financial incentives or rewards. These incentives or rewards can be helpful in providing positive motivation to the VEDC members and help boost the morale of the VEDCs members and develop a feeling of belongingness among the members towards their school.
5. ***Decreasing Workload of the Secretary:*** The work load of the Secretary should be lessened. As per the Guidelines, the head teacher is entrusted with all the responsibilities ranging from nominations of VEDC members to maintaining the accounts and records of this body. He has to convene the meetings, record the minutes and not only this, he is the one who has to compile and submit all the progress reports to the appropriate authorities all by himself. It is the sole responsibility of the secretary to maintain the accounts and get all SSA activities completed as per norms. This is something too much for one individual who is simultaneously expected to take care of general administration of the school apart from taking the classes. Thus the study recommends that as the burden

on the head teacher is too much, there is a need to unburden him by providing a helping hand.

6. ***Ensure Regular Periodic Trainings*:** Periodic trainings are very important for increasing the awareness (thereby the performance) of the members on procedures followed for nominations, formation and functions of VEDCs. The trainings can further improve the functioning of these bodies and the standards of school education at the village level. As per the Guidelines, periodic trainings are an important component for capacity building of VEDCs members, however, the survey revealed that hardly any training on regular basis is held for the VEDC members.

Bibliography

Aggarwal, D.D. 2002. *History and Development of Elementary Education in India*. New Delhi: Sarup and Sons.

Aggarwal, Yash. 1999. *Trends in Access and Retention*. New Delhi: National Institute of Educational Planning and Administration. New Delhi: NIEPA.

Aikara, Jacob. 2011. "Decentralization of Elementary Education and Community Participation in Kerala". *Rajgiri Journal of Social Development*. Vol 2(2). June. pp161-194

Azim Premji Foundation. 2004. *Social Context of Elementary Education in Rural India*. Bangalore.

Banerjee, Abhijit. et. al. 2007. "Can Information Campaigns Raise Awareness and Local Participation in Primary Education?" *Economic and Political Weekly*. April 14. p 1365-72

Basudeo, Y. 1987. *A Study on Community Participation in Education Development Programme at School Level in District Ballia of U.P.* New Delhi: NUEPA.

Beyene, Y., Gaumnitz, A., Goike, C. and Robbins, T., 2005. *Stimulating Community Participation in Primary Schools: Perspectives on the Basic Education Strategic Objective Program II (BESO II) Project in Bahir Dar, Ethiopia*. World Learning for International Development. The George Washington University, Washington, D.C.

Bhargava, B.S. 1979. *Grass Roots Leadership: A Study of Leadership in PRIs*. Ashish Publishing House. New Delhi.

Bhattacharjya, Saradi. 2001. *Functioning of Village Education Committee: A Study of Selected VECs in Ghunucha Cluster of Morigaon District, Assam*. New Delhi: NUEPA.

Bjork, Christopher. 2006. Educational *Decentralization: Asian Experiences and Conceptual Contributions*. Volume 8. Springer Netherlands.

Bobekova, Elvira. 2007. *Decentralization of Education in Rural Kyrgyzstan*. Online Available at http://www.adb.org/AnnualMeeting/2007/Essay-Competition/winning-entries/Elvira-Bobekova.pdf. Retrieved on Feb 01, 2010.

CED (Centre for Education and Documentation). 2005. Non-Formal Education-Information database in the Asia-Pacific Region. CED code R. No. 30.9. Online available at < http://www.doccentre.net>

Chaturvedi, Abhisek. 2003. 'Indian Experiments with Decentralized Governance'. *The Ritinjali Journal*. Online available at < www.ritinjali.org/articles/abhisek.htm>

Dash, B.K. 1983. *A Study of the Impact of Community Participation in the Universalisation of Primary Education*. New Delhi: NUEPA.

Dash, Ranjan Kumar and Panda, B.N. 2009. "Effectiveness of Village Education Committee on Promoting Universal Elementary Education: A Case Study". *E-Journal of All India Association of Educational Research*. Vol. 21(1). June. Online available at http://www.ejournal.aiaer.net/.

Duggal, Janak. 1993. "Access of Scheduled Caste Girls to Elementary Education in Rural Haryana: A Study of Socio-Economic Problems in Universalisation of Elementary Education". An unpublished Ph.D. Thesis. Faculty of Education. New Delhi: Jamia Millia Islamia.

ED.CIL. 2000. *District Primary Education Programme, Research Abstract in Primary Education (1994-2000)*. New Delhi.

ED.CIL. 2002. *District Primary Education Programme, Research Abstract in Primary Education (1999-2002)*. New Delhi.

Education and Technology Services Limited. 2007. *Computer Assisted Learning Programme for Village Education Committee (VEC): Impact Analysis Report*. Online available at: www.ilfsets.com

Eldah Nyamoita Onsomu, John Njoroge Mungai, Dramane Oulai, James Sankale, Jeddidah Mujidi. 2004. "Community schools in Kenya: Case study on community participation in funding and managing schools". International Institute for Educational Planning. UNESCO.

Ghosh, Avik. 2004. "Alternative Schools and Education Guarantee Scheme" In Vimala Ramachadran (ed.). *Gender and Social Equity in Primary Education*. New Delhi: Sage. p129.

Government of India. 1986. *National Policy on Education 1986*. Ministry of Human Resource Development, Department of Education, New Delhi,

Government of India. 1992. *Report of the CABE Committee on Policy*, Department of Education, Ministry of HRD: New Delhi.

Government of India. Ministry of Education. 1954. Report on the Committee on Relationship between State Governments and Local Bodies in the Administration of Primary Education 1954. Online available at <www.education.nic.in/cd50years/g/52/4M/524M0101.htm

Government of India. Ministry of Education. 1966. Report of the Education Commission 1964–66: Education and National Development. Delhi.

Gopalan K. 1998. *Indian Strategies to Achieve Universalisation of Elementary Education*. Indira Gandhi National Centre for the Arts: New Delhi. Online available at < http://ignca.nic.in/cd_06019.htm>

Government of India. 1986. *Programme of Action: National Policy on Education* 1986. Ministry of Human Resource Development, Department of Education: New Delhi.

Government of India. 2005. *National Curriculum Framework 2005,* National Council of Educational Research and Training: New Delhi, December 2005.

Government of India. 2010. *Compilation of 50 years of Indian Education: 1947-1997.* Online available at <http://www. education.nic.in/cd50years/home.htm>.

Government of India. 2000. *Sarva Shiksha Abhiyan: A Programme for Universal Elementary Education-Framework for Implementation,* Ministry of Human Resource Development, Department of Elementary Education and Literacy: New Delhi.

Government of India. Ministry of Education. 1997. District Primary Education Programme Guidelines. NCERT: New Delhi.

Government of India. Ministry of Human Resource Management. 2002. "Janshala: Towards Empowered Community Schools". New Delhi. Online available at < http://www.education.nic.in/Janshala/contents/pdf>

Government of Karnataka. SERT. 2004. *A Study to Evaluate the Functioning of School Development and Monitoring Committees in Karnataka.* Bangalore.

Government of Maharashtra. 2009 School Education and Sport Department. *Mid-day Meal in Schools (MDM) Annual Work Plan and Budget Document 2009-10*

Govinda, R. 2002. "Dynamics of Decentralized management in Primary Education: Policy and Practice in Rajasthan and Madhya Pradesh. In R. Govinda and Rashmi Diwan (eds.), *Community Participation and Empowerment in Primary Education,* Sage Publication: New Delhi.

Govinda, R and Rashmi, Diwan (eds). 2007. *Community Participation and Empowerment in Primary Education.* New Delhi: Sage.

Govinda, R. and N.V. Varghese. 1991. *The Quality of Basic Education Services in India: A Case Study of Primary Schooling in Madhya Pradesh,* National Institute of Educational Planning and Administration: New Delhi.

Govinda, R. 1999. *Reaching the Unreached through Participatory Planning: Study of School mapping in Lok Jumbhish.* Paris: International Institute of Educational Planning. UNESCO.

Government of Punjab. Sarva Shiksha Abhiyan Authority. undated. *Guidelines for Maintaining Accounts under Village Education Development Committees.* Chandigarh.

Government of Punjab. Sarva Shiksha Abhiyan Authority. undated. *How the Construction Works are to be done under Village Education Development Committees?.* Chandigarh.

Government of Punjab. Sarva Shiksha Abhiyan Authority. undated. *Norms for Village Education Development Committees.* Chandigarh.

Government of Punjab. Sarva Shiksha Abhiyan Authority. undated. *Guidelines for Rural/Urban Education Development Committees*. Chandigarh.

Gowda. K.G. 1990. *Generation and Sustenance of Community Participation in Development of Primary Education: A Study to Review the Role of Community in Promoting Primary Education in Komalapura Mandal Panchayat Area, Periapatna Taluk. Mysore District, Karnataka*. New Delhi: NUEPA.

Haq, M. Nazmul. 1996. "Status of Community Involvement in Primary Education in Bangladesh". Institute of Education and Research. University of Dhaka, Dhaka. A paper presented at the combined conference of the Education Association and Australian Association for Research in Education, Singapore. November.

Hill, Franklin. 2005. *Community Involvement – Is It Rinky-dink or a Chance to Think?*. Online available at <http://www.schoolfacilities.com/cd_1679.aspx.>, Retrieved on Feb 01, 2010.

Institute of Rural Research and Development. 2010. *Report on Capacity-Building Needs: Village Education Committee*. Gurgaon. July

Juyal R P and Singh, Manjit. 2007. *Baseline Social Assessment Study of Elementary Education in Punjab. District Mansa*. National Institute of Administrative Research. LBSNAA. Mussoorie. Unpublished Reports.

Juyal, R.P., Singh, D.P. 2007. *Baseline Social Assessment Study – District Ferozepur and Moga, Punjab*. Mussoorie: NIAR. (Unpublished Reports).

Kantha, Vinay and Narain, Daisy. 2002 "Dynamics of Community Participation in a Fragmented and Turbulent State". In R. Govinda and Rashmi Diwan (eds.), *Community Participation and Empowerment in Primary Education*, Sage Publication: New Delhi.

Kapadia, K.M. 1966. *Marriage and Family in India*. Oxford University Press: London.

Kumar, S., Patel, R.C., Mehta Anjali. 1999. "Community Participation in Primary Education". *The School Teacher*. Vol. 24(4), October.

Kumar, Sanjeev. 2005. *Community Participation in Elementary Education*. New Delhi: Indian Publishers and Distributors.

Lal, Manohar. 1997. *Community Participation through Village Education Committee (VEC) in Primary Education in Selected Blocks of Sitamarhi District in Bihar*. New Delhi: NUEPA.

Mallik, S.K., 1996." Education under Panchayats: Quantitative and Qualitative Dimensions". *Man and Development*. XVIII (3), 46 -53.

Mehta, Arun C. 2005. *Elementary Education in Unrecognized Schools in India*. New Delhi: National Institute of Educational Planning and Administration.

Menon, Pramila. 1996. "Towards Educating a Community: An Action Research Experience". *Progressive Educational Herald*. July.

Menon, Pramila. 1999. *Functioning of Village Education Committee: A Study of Haryana*. New Delhi: NUEPA.

Ministry of HRD. Department of School Education and Literacy. 2008. *Sarva Shiksha Abhiyan: Framework for Implementation: 2008.*

Mizzammil, M. 1998. "Community Participation and Resource Mobilsation for Educational Development of Minorities". In Ved Prakash (ed.) *Studies on Learning Organizations, Community Participation and School Effectiveness at Primary Stage.* New Delhi: NCERT.

Mohan, Shantha, N., Dutt, Gayatri Devi, M.D and Antony, Piush. 2003. "Community Participation in Primary Education". In R. Govinda and Rashmi Diwan (eds.), *Community Participation and Empowerment in Primary Education.* Sage Publication: New Delhi.

Mohanty, S.K. 1999. *Community Participation in Relation to School Effectiveness in DPEP and Non – DPEP District in Haryana.* Unpublished M. Phil. (Education) Dissertation: Kurukshetra University, Kurukshetra.

Mohanty, S.K. 2003. *Impact of Early Childhood Education on Enrolment, Retention and Scholastic Achievement of Rural Primary School Children of Haryana.* Unpublished Doctoral Thesis, Kurukshetra University, Kurukshetra.

Mor, D.P. 2008. "Encourage Community Participation". *The Tribune.* April 29. Online available at <http://www.tribuneindia.com/2008/20080429/edu. htm #2>

Narayana, M. and Chandrakant. 2000. *Functioning of VEC in Satra District of Maharashtra: A Study in Reference to Adult Education.* Unpublished Dissertation. NUEPA: New Delhi.

Nayak, P.M. 2009. *Community Participation in the Universalisation of Primary Education.* New Delhi: Academic Excellence Publishers and Distributors.

NIEPA.1997. *Planning Process under DPEP: National Level.* New Delhi.

Noronha, Anjali. 2003. 'The Community in Charge: Shades of Experience form Madhya Pradesh', in R. Govinda and Rashmi Diwan (eds.), *Community Participation and Empowerment in Primary Education.* Sage Publication: New Delhi.

Palakshiah. 1999. *Community Mobilization for Effective Functioning of Schools in Tiptur Taluk of Tumkur District in Karnataka.* New Delhi: NUEPA.

Pandey, P. Goyal, S. Sundararaman, V. 2008. "Community Participation in Public Schools: The Impact of Information Campaigns in Three Indian States". Policy Research Working Paper, 4776. *The World Bank.* South Asia Region. Human Development Department. November.

Parajuli, Mahesh Nath. 2007. "People's Participation in School Governance? Realities of Educational Decentralization in Nepal" in Daun, Holger (ed.). *School Decentralization in the Context of Globalizing Governance: International Comparison of Grassroots Responses*: Springer. 195-211.

Planning Commision of India. 1994. *Bihar Education Project-Report of the Review-cum-Appraisal Mission 1994.* Online Available at

<planningcommission.nic.in/reports/sereports/ser/.../stdy-berchi.pdf.>

Planning Commission of India 2007 Tenth Five Year Plan (2002-2007) Document. (Chapter 4.1). New Delhi.

Ramachandran, Vimala. 2001. 'Community Participation in Primary Education: Innovations in Rajasthan'. *Economic and Political Weekly*. XXXVI (25). June 23.

Ramachandran, Vimala and Sethi, Harsh. 2000. Rajasthan Shiksha Karmi Project. An Appraisal. New Education Divison. Document No. 7. SIDA, Embassy of Sweden. New Delhi.

Rani, Celine A. 2002. *Emerging Pattern of Rural Women Leadership in India*. Kalpaz Publications. Delhi.

Rani, Raj and Arora, Ranjana. 2004. 'Community Participation in Elementary Education'. *The Primary Teacher*, July and October.

Rao, Vasanta Srinivasa. 2008. "Primary Education in Tribal areas: A Study of Community Participation under Sarva Shiksha Abhiyan". A Ph.D. Dissertation. Andhra University.

Rao, Vasanta Srinivasa. 2009. "Lack of Community Participation in the Sarva Shiksha Abhiyan: A Case Study". *Economic and Political Weekly*. Vol. XLIV (8). February 21.

Rao, N.M. 1998. "Combating School Dysfunctional between Community Mobilizations: Case Study of a Rural School". In Ved Prakash (ed.), *Studies on Learning Organization, Community Participation and School Effectiveness at Primary Stage*. New Delhi: NCERT.

Rashid, S.M.A. and Salam, Abdus. 1999."Village Development Committees-Holistic Progress." *Paper* presented in 25th WEDC Conference on Integrated Water Supply and Sanitation. Addis Ababa. Ethiopia.

Sahu, T.K. 2002. *Concept and Existing Practice of Teachers' Accountability in Secondary Schools of Haryana-An Evaluative Study*. Unpublished Doctoral Thesis: Kurukshetra University, Kurukshetra.

Shaeffer, Sheldon. 1991. *A Framework for Collaborating for Educational Change, Increasing and Improving the Quality of Basic Education*. Monograph No. 3. Paris: International Institute of Educational Planning.

Shankar Girija, K. 2008. 'Community Involvement in Sarva Shiksha Abhiyan: An Assessment of the Village Education Committees in India'. *Madhya Pradesh Journal of Social Sciences*. Vol. 13(1):75-88

Shilu, A.O. 1995. *Role of the Village Education Committee in Planning and Management of Primary Education: A Case Study of Kohima District of Nagaland*. New Delhi: NUEPA.

Singh, Abhimanyu. 1999. Fifty Years of Elementary Education. Online available at <http://www.un.org.in/JANSHALA/jan1999/default.htm>

Singh, D.R. 1985. *Rural Leadership among Scheduled Castes*. Chug Publications. Allahabad.

Singh, Manjit and Choudhary, R.K. 2007. *Baseline Social Assessment Study of Elementary Education in Punjab. District Muktsar*. National Institute of Administrative Research. LBSNAA. Mussoorie. Unpublished Reports.

Sinha, Sujit. 2007. "Community Participation in Primary Schools: Experiments by Swanirvar in North 24 Parganas of West Bengal". Online Available on www.solutionexchange-un.net.in/education/.../res-10-030907-02.doc. Retrieved on Feb 02, 2010

Srinivas, M.N. 1959. "The Dominant Castes in Rampura". *American Anthropologist*. Vol. 61. No.1. p61.

Srinivas, M.N. 1962. *Caste in Modern India and Other Essays*. Asia Publishing House. Bombay.

Sujatha, K. and Rao, M.S. 2000. *Community Participation in Education in Tribal Areas: Study of Maabadies (Community Schools) in Visakhapatnam District of Andhra Pradesh*. Unpublished Dissertation. NIEPA: New Delhi.

The International City/County Management Association IQ Report. 2008. *Local Governments and Schools: A Community-Oriented Approach*, Vol. 40, Special Edition, Capitol St., NE, Suite 500, Washington, DC.

Tom-Miura, Allison. 2004. *Engaging Communities in the Planning of New Urban Public Schools*, Doctoral Dissertation, University of Southern California, Los Angeles, December.

Tongpangshilu. 1990. *Constitution of Village Education Committee and its Responsibilities for Promotion of Primary Education in Nagaland: A Study of Mokokchung District*. New Delhi: NUEPA.

Tyagi, R.S. 1999. "Role of Village Education Committees in Improvement of Community Participation in Education", *Journal of Educational Planning and Administration*, Research Note, Vol. XIII (3), July.

UNICEF. 2011. *Schools of Quality: A Case Study on Rights-Based Education Reform in the Lao People's Democratic Republic*. Vientiane. March

USAID 2005. *Community Participation Key to Improving Schools*. Online Available. <http://africastories.usaid.gov/search_details.cfm?story ID=339&countryID=14&sectorID=0&yearID=5> Retrieved on Feb 10, 2010.

Vaijayanti K. 2005. *Involving the Community in Elementary Education: Role of School Development and Monitoring Committee*. Policy Planning Unit, Azim Premji Foundation, Bangalore.

Varghese, N.V. and A.C. Mehta. 1999. *Universalisation of Upper Primary Education in India: An Analysis of School Facilities and their Cost Implications*. NIEPA: New Delhi.

Varghese, N.V., undated. "Decentralization of Educational Planning and DPEP". (Unpublished paper). NIEPA: New Delhi.

Vimala, Ramachadran 2004. *Gender and Social Equity in Primary Education*. New Delhi: Sage.

Vimala, Ramachadran. 2001. "Community Participation in Primary Education: Innovations in Rajasthan". *Economic Political Weekly*. June 23.

Wankhede, G.G. and Sengupta, Anirban. 2005. "Village Education Committees in West Bengal, India: Planned Vision and Beyond". *International Journal of Educational Development*. Vol. 25. (2005): 569–579

Yadav, R.S. 2006. *Community Participation in Education: Role of VECs in Haryana*. Associated Publishers: Ambala Cantt

Zingkhai, Apam and Asung, R. 2011. "SMC in Manipur–School Management Committee or State Managed Corruption?" *The Sangai Express*. July 06.

Index

73rd and 74th Constitution Amendments Acts, 7–8, 10, 13

Absenteeism, 11
Accelerated Rural Water Supply Programme, 116
Accountability, 14, 17, 22, 52, 66, 120
Acharya Ramamurti Committee, 11–12
Actual Payee Receipt (APR), 74
Adult education instructors, 59
Anganwadi programmes, 70
Ashok Mehta Committee, 10–11
Attitudinal change of villagers, 40, 61
Awareness scale, 109, 164

Balwant Rai Mehta Committee, 9
Barrier-free education policy formulation, 69
Basic Education Strategic Objective Program II, 50
Bihar Education Project (BEP), 16–17, 28, 58
Bihar State Vidyalaya Shiksha Samiti Act, 58
Block Education officer (BEO), 17, 26, 58, 65, 75, 81–82
Block Resource Centre, 27
Block Resource Persons (BRPs), 89
Broad Strategies Central to Sarva Shiksha Abhiyan Programme, 21

Caste-based provisions of reservation, absence of, 104, 161
Caste-class composition, 3
Celebrations of national days, 27, 143
Centralization of education, 1, 6
Child-friendly Schools, 54
Civil society, 16, 25, 36, 45, 116, 158, 160
    elements, 45
    participation, 45
Cluster Resource Centre (CRC), 23, 27–28, 74–75, 81, 83
Cluster Resource Persons (CRPs), 89
Community anchors, 54
Community cohesion, 54
Community development, 9, 49
Community education assessment, 51
Community engagement practices, 49
Community funds, 30, 59
Community participation movement, 1, 4
Community participation projects, 49
Community-based information, 22
Community-based institutions, 56
Community-oriented schools, 54
Compulsory Primary Education Act, 5
Congress Government, 68, 121
Corpus fund, 33
Cost saving policy, 52
Cultural programme, 84, 96, 111, 142, 166, 170
Culture factors, 100, 161
Curriculum-related material development, 23

Decentralization of education, 1, 10, 24, 45, 51–52, 64, 159
Decentralized decision, effective system of, 2, 20, 25, 158
Decentralized model of development, 26, 65–66
Decentralized planning, 2, 12, 19, 67
Department of Audit, 76
Department of Drinking Water Supply, 116
Department of School Education and Sport, 41
Deprived children, 68
Developmental activities, 73

Disadvantaged groups, 16, 20–22, 37, 62, 67
Display board, 76, 80, 156
District Elementary Education Plans, 23
District Information System on Education, 113
District level institutions, 21
District Planning and Development Board, 82
District Primary Education Programme, 25
District Primary Education Project (DPEP), 18–19, 25, 27, 29, 32
District Resource Persons (DRPs), 89
Dominant castes, 104, 162
Dowry system, 47
Drinking water facilities, 35, 115–16, 162

Dropout, 35, 62, 130
Early Childhood Care and Education (ECCE), 21
Education Commission, 1, 24
Education Development Committees, 87
Education Development Index, 120, 175
Education for All (EFA), 1, 5, 7–10, 16, 48, 55, 153, 173
Education for self-development, 7
Education of Girls, Priority to, 22
Education system
  centralized, 52
  dual, 10
  formal, 7, 48
  prevalent, 21
Education
  basic, 15, 20, 48, 54
  finance, 52
  formal, 43–44, 159
  joyful, 70
  quality of, 6, 11, 37, 43, 48, 50–52, 54, 66, 85, 98, 120, 153, 164, 175
  universal, 36
Educational Development Index (EDI), 113
Educational governance, 13
Educational intervention, 30, 59
Educational Management Information System (EMIS), 22
Educational tours, 84, 96
Elementary education sector, 23
Elementary education, 6–9, 19–21, 32, 38, 45, 70–71, 73, 81–82, 93–95, 107, 110, 113, 138, 140, 159
  compulsory, 10
  quality issue of, 38, 159
  communitisation of, 6
  goal of universalisation of, 4, 8, 67
  management of, 1–2, 24
  Universalisation of, 9, 19
  universal, 5, 15, 20–21, 40
Elementary schools, 21, 66, 87, 141
Employment generation schemes, 35, 63
Ethiopian schools, 49

Financial incentives, 147–48, 171, 175
First aid kits, 119–20, 163
Free education policy framework, 48
Fundraising activities, 140, 156, 169
Funds/donations, 133, 155, 168

Gandhi's approach, 7–8
Gender-sensitive methods, 19
General Impression of Teachers, 152
Girls' Advisory Committees, 50
Gram Panchayat meetings, 33
Gram sabha meetings, 76, 98
Gram Sansad, meeting of, 35, 63
Grant/funds, 72–73, 78, 83–84, 111, 166
Guidance services, 34

Head teacher of school, 72
High literacy villages, 89, 104, 122–23, 125–27, 130, 140–41, 166–67
High-quality education, 54
Hussein, Zakir, 7
Hygiene practices, 46–47

Inclusion of minorities, 15
Institute of Rural Research and Development, 43, 111, 159
Institutional capacities, 37, 85
Institutional Capacity Building, 21
Institutional reforms, 21, 68
Institutionalized structures, 28
Intellectual development, 96
Interpersonal communication, 47

Janardhana Reddy Committee, 12

Janshala Programme, 19
Jomtien Declaration, 1
Judo karate workshops, 140–41
Kher Committee, 9

Legal education framework, 48
Local Construction Committees (LCC), 72, 78, 80
Local development functionaries, 59
Local management committees, 68
Local self-government institutions, 2, 24, 101
Lok Jumbish (LJ), 25, 17–18
Los Angeles Unified School District (LAUSD), 49
Low literacy villages, 89, 104, 123–27, 130, 133, 139, 141, 166–67

Mahila Mandals, 41, 64–65
Management systems, 41, 69
  hierarchical, 18
  participatory, 16
Mass education, 7, 9
Mid day meals, 30, 32, 39–41, 43, 63–64, 67, 98, 119–20, 148, 163, 172
Monitoring mechanism, 32, 56, 62, 159
Mothers Teachers Associations (MTAs), 6, 18–19, 21, 56, 65
National Curriculum Framework (NCF), 7, 13
National Education Commission, 9
National Literacy Mission Programme, 16
National Policy on Education (NPE), 2, 6–7, 10–13, 24
Needy children, 84
Non-formal education, 48
Non-teaching staff salaries, 48
Out-of-school children, 95–97, 121, 137, 140–41

Panchayati Raj Institutions (PRIs), 2–3, 13–14, 19–21, 24, 28–29, 31, 42, 56, 60, 67–68, 86
Parents Teachers Associations (PTA), 6, 25, 27, 33, 35, 38–39, 46, 51, 56, 65, 92–94, 106–7, 110, 165, 174
Parents-Teachers Associations, 19, 21, 25, 27, 33, 35, 37–38, 51, 59, 65–66, 85, 87, 92
Participation of children, 20, 22, 27
Participatory Management of Schools, 67
Participatory processes, 17–18, 140
Pendu Sikhiya Vikas Committees, 68
Planning Commission, 16–17, 19
Post Literacy Campaigns, 16
Poverty alleviation programme, 35, 63
Primary education, 3–4, 9, 16–19, 24, 26–29, 31, 36, 42, 46, 48, 50, 54, 61–62, 153
  development of, 30, 68
  improvement of, 41, 61
  management of, 42, 61, 153
  qualitative improvement of, 42, 61
  universalisation of, 42, 61
Private-Aided Schools, 41, 64
Progress reports, 74, 81, 85, 95, 146, 175

Quality education, 25, 49
Quality schooling, 55

Rajasthan Lok Jumbhish, 17
Reddy committee, 11
Regular attendance of children, 31, 155
Religious organization, 146, 171
Remedial/coaching classes, 140
Representation of women, 26, 58, 100
Resource groups, 29
Retention of children, 19, 60
Right to Education Act, 2, 7, 23, 25, 158

Sarva Shiksha Abhiyan (SSA), 2, 13, 20–23, 25, 39–40, 43, 59, 66–68, 71, 86–87, 97, 116–17, 119, 138–41, 157–58
Sarva Shiksha Abhiyan, 39, 68, 90, 93–95, 97, 134, 141, 160, 168
School buildings, 34, 39, 62, 83, 96, 114–16, 119, 139, 162
  condition of, 115
  construction of, 55, 146
  new, 30
  primary, 64
School construction programs, 49
School Development and Management Committees (SDMCs), 32–33, 39, 62, 103, 159
School improvement plans, 43, 55, 59
School magazines, 27, 143
School Management Committees, 2, 8, 21, 23, 25, 41–42, 44–45, 53, 64, 86, 158

School-community partnerships, 37, 85
Schooling facilities, 5
School-related activities, 43, 59
Schools of Quality (SoQ), 10, 54–55
Secondary education, 13, 48
Self Help Groups, 41, 64
Shiksha Karmi Project (SKP), 15–16, 25
Single classroom schools, 113
Single teacher schools, 43
Special education facilities, 70
Special Groups, 22
Sports activities, 133, 142, 168
Sports days, 27, 143
State-civil society partnerships, 45
Stock register, 74, 80
Swedish International Development Cooperation Agency, 15
Systematic mobilization, 2, 20, 25, 158

Teacher-pupil ratio, 27, 32
Teaching learning environment, 57, 133
Teaching Learning Material (TLM), 32, 37, 39–41, 61, 96, 119, 136–37, 139, 169
Teaching learning strategies, effective, 22
Teaching material, low cost, 27
Teaching-learning environment, 143
Technology savvy parents, 50
Total Literacy Campaigns, 16
Total Sanitation Campaign (TSC), 116
Tribal Autonomous Councils, 21

UNESCO Delhi Declaration, 1
UNICEF, 19, 54
Universal Elementary Education (UEE), 5, 9, 15, 20–21, 23, 25, 40, 158
University of Southern California, 49
Urban Slum level Education Committees, 21
USAID, 50–51
Utilization of Funds, Approval for, 77
Vidyalaya Shiksha Samiti (VSS), 57
Village community, 6, 25, 42, 104, 159, 162
Village Construction Committee (VCC), 27
Village Development Boards, 64
Village Development Committees (VDCs), 46–47
Village education committee meetings, 16
Village Education Committees (VECs), 2–3, 11–12, 16–20, 24–31, 34–41, 43–44, 56–66, 68, 85–86, 95, 100, 112, 143, 151, 159–60
  constitution of, 2, 5, 24
  minimum qualification of president of, 30, 60
  process of formation of, 26, 58
  role of, 31
  tribal school, 41
Village Education Development Committees (VEDC), 6, 37, 55, 67–68, 85–87, 90, 92–93, 102, 105, 108, 110, 113, 120–21, 150–51, 166
  activities of, 154–55, 173
  composition of, 69, 92, 105–7, 145, 171
  contribution of, 133, 136, 140, 143, 151, 154, 156–57, 168, 170, 172, 174
  functions of, 92, 95, 98–99, 110–12, 157, 176
  goals of, 69
  major focus of, 137, 169
  performance of, 153, 173
  preamble of, 69
  process of formation of, 107–8, 164
  progress reports of, 74
  responsibilities of, 78
  sources of income of, 82
  tenure of, 71, 95
Village education plan, 29, 43, 59
Village education register, 29
Village Educational Committees, 25, 66, 158
Village panchayat, 68, 70, 87, 92, 105, 107, 110, 117, 165
Village-based campaign, 36
Vocational education, 32
Voluntary organizations, 10, 18, 28, 65
Volunteer teachers, 16

Ward Education Committees (WECs), 25, 41, 64, 158
Watson programme, 46–47
Women representatives, 68
World Bank, 25
World Conference on Education, 1

Zilla Parishads, 11